DON'T MISS OUT ON ANY OF

SPARKNOTES®
SAT VOCABULARY NOVELS

BUSTED

HEAD OVER HEELS

RAVE NEW WORLD

SUN-KISSED

VAMPIRE DREAMS

n-

sed

AN SAT VOCABULARY NOVEL

BY BELINDA RAY

SPARK
NOTES

SPARKNOTES is a registered trademark of SparkNotes LLC

Spark Publishing
A Division of Barnes & Noble Publishing
120 Fifth Avenue
New York, NY 10011
www.sparknotes.com

SAT is a registered trademark of the College Entrance Examination Board, which was not involved in the production of, and does not endorse, this book.

ISBN-13: 978-1-4114-0080-1
ISBN-10: 1-4114-0080-1

Please submit all questions or comments or report errors to
www.sparknotes.com/errors

Printed and bound in the United States

Library of Congress Cataloging-in-Publication Data:

Ray, Belinda.
    Sun-kissed : an SAT vocabulary novel / by Belinda Ray.
        p. cm. — (An SAT vocabulary novel)
    Summary: A counseling group and surfing in New Hampshire's winter waves help high school junior Kristen Carmichael deal with her parents' divorce and new relationships after she makes some very bad choices at school and with her friends.
    ISBN 1-4114-0080-1
    [1. Family problems—Fiction. 2. Interpersonal relations—Fiction. 3. Surfing—Fiction. 4. High schools—Fiction. 5. Schools—Fiction. 6. Divorce—Fiction.]
    I. Title. II. SAT vocabulary novels
    PZ7.R210115Su 2004
    [Fic]—dc22   2004000313

Algebra II *in*, American History *out*. French IV *out*, British Lit *in*.

Kristen Carmichael **shuffled** textbooks between her backpack and her locker, shifting and **rearranging**, wondering why she'd even bothered to bring any of the books home. She hadn't opened a single one all weekend—hadn't unzipped her backpack once. Instead, she'd plunked it in the corner of her bedroom at her father's house on Friday night, where it had sat, untouched—except for when she'd removed her *Longboard* magazine from the side mesh pocket—until Monday morning, at which point she'd hefted it onto her shoulder and hopped into her dad's BMW for the forty-five-minute **commute** to John Quincy Adams High.

Lately, the teal L.L. Bean backpack she'd had since seventh grade had served Kristen better as a dumbbell than book bag. Her muscles were getting stronger from toting it around, but her brain certainly wasn't **reaping** any benefits. Not that it mattered. She was just doing seat time. The bag was simply a prop, preventing her from being too conspicuous in class, so she could sit in her chair undetected with all the right materials present.

And it didn't hurt that Kristen's backpack was the *right* backpack. It wasn't too worn, too new, too flashy, too different—nothing that attracted attention. The teal color was common enough without being boring, and L.L. Bean was a respectably traditional brand.

Kristen's clothing followed a similar vein. Her low-rise jeans and Billabong tee were stylishly chic, her jaggedly parted, bone-straight blond hair just as fashionable and cutting edge as that of every teen model gazing out from a magazine cover in the checkout line. She blended seamlessly into current pop culture, fortunate enough to

---

shuffled: shifted **commute**: trip **reaping**: obtaining
rearranging: adjusting

have been born with decent fashion sense and a slim body shape, two things that had **ensured** her a spot in the popular crowd since fourth grade.

Of course, now, in her junior year of high school, being part of the popular crowd carried many more responsibilities than it had when she was nine years old. There were all kinds of **rituals** she had to worry about. There were people to talk to, others to avoid, and it was important to be seen in the right places, show up at the right parties, wear the right clothes, date within the right circle, get decent grades without working too hard, and follow the latest trends without getting too far ahead or falling too far behind.

Somehow, **despite** all of the rules involved in being popular and Kristen's **waning** interest in keeping up with them, she had managed to remain part of the social elite, an accomplishment that, in high school, was both a blessing and a curse.

Kristen snagged her chemistry book from her top locker shelf and jammed it into her backpack, finally ready to set out for her morning classes. She was just about to head down the hall when she felt a tap on her shoulder.

"Hey—what happened to you Saturday night?"

Kristen winced at the sound of her best friend, Leah McDonnell's, voice. She'd been dreading this moment all morning long. In fact, she'd been thinking about it with **trepidation** since Saturday afternoon, when she'd decided that hitting the surf on Sunday was more important than hitting the party that night. It hadn't been a tough choice, although she'd known she'd eventually have to find a way to answer for her absence at the most recent drunk-fest without sounding too pleased about having missed it, as that would only **alienate** Leah further.

"I thought you were going to meet us over at my house and head to the party from there," Leah said.

---

ensured: assured   **despite:** notwithstanding   **trepidation:** fear
rituals: routines   **waning:** dwindling   **alienate:** antagonize

Kristen took a deep breath. "I meant to meet you," she started, "but—"

"I tried your house like five times before we left, and there was no answer," Leah broke in. "Of course I wanted to wait, because I knew you wouldn't ditch us for no good reason, and I was kind of worried that something had happened to you, but Tracy was all, 'If we don't leave right now, we're going to miss the whole party'—you know how she gets. So I figured I'd just take a chance and go and hope that you would meet us there, but you never showed. Why didn't your answering machine pick up, anyway?"

"Huh?" Kristen asked, squinting. Leah talked faster than any other human being on earth, and sometimes their conversations—or rather, Leah's **soliloquies**—left Kristen feeling a bit spun.

"Your answering machine," Leah repeated. "It never picked up, and I let the phone ring like fifteen times."

"Oh, right," Kristen said. "I forgot to tell you—my mom's machine broke last Thursday, and she hasn't had time to get a new one yet. She started her new job at KJKF on Friday, so she's been at the station nonstop."

"So then why didn't you—?"

"Hey, Carmichael—where were you Saturday?" Trevor Wilson called as he headed toward them. "Too good to party with your **plebeian** friends or something?" As he walked by, he flashed Kristen a smile that would have knocked half the female population of Adams High flat. Kristen still felt the smallest twinge of the heart flutter she would have had in the past—before everything had changed. But it was so much harder now to care about a guy like Trevor flirting with her. Any guy, actually.

"He asked about you, you know," Leah said, smiling sideways at Kristen.

"Really?" Kristen asked.

"Mm-hmm. *Twice.*"

---

soliloquies: monologues   **plebeian:** commonplace

"Wow," Kristen said, drawing the word out in an attempt to sound **sincere**. "That's amazing. So . . . who did he hook up with when he realized I wasn't around?"

"Kristen!"

"Oh, come on, Leah. Everyone knows he's a dog. He'll take whoever's available."

"Do you think he knows *I'm* available?" Leah asked, watching as Trevor opened his locker at the other end of the hall.

Kristen followed her friend's dreamy gaze and **grimaced**. "Please. You can do *way* better than him, Leah."

"Better than gorgeous, smart, and funny? Better than MVP of the football team and vice president of the student council? Are you high?"

"No, but it sounds like you are," Kristen said. "Trevor's a jerk—he's totally stuck on himself. You'd be better off dating Mike Leding."

Leah narrowed her eyes. "Mike Leding's *gay*," she protested.

"Yep, and he'd make a better boyfriend."

"Better than who?"

Kristen whirled around to see Tracy Parks and Stephanie Baker standing behind her.

"Who are you guys talking about?" Tracy asked, glancing from Kristen to Leah and back again. Kristen tried to shrug the question off, but Leah was all too happy to volunteer information.

"Kristen thinks that Mike Leding would be a better boyfriend than Trevor," she said. Tracy and Stephanie both squinted at Kristen like she'd just **nominated** Charles Manson for a Nobel Peace Prize.

"Isn't Mike Leding gay?" Stephanie asked.

"Yes," Kristen said, giving them a sly smile. "**Blatantly**. That's the point."

"Not this again." Tracy moaned, shaking her head.

---

sincere: real, genuine   **nominated:** recommended   **blatantly:** obviously
grimaced: frowned

"What's that supposed to mean?" Kristen asked.

Tracy let out a sigh and shifted her weight so that her right hip jutted out **indignantly.** "It means that your anti-Trevor act is getting old."

Kristen's eyebrows shot up. "My anti-Trevor act?"

"I know what's going on," Tracy said. "He likes you and you know it, so you're acting all **aloof,** stringing him along to see just how far he'll go for you and how much attention you can get out of the whole thing."

Tracy's logic was so warped that Kristen wasn't sure how to respond at first, but finally she found her voice. "I'm not stringing him along," she said, her words slow and measured. "And if it seems like I'm playing hard to get, it's probably because I'm not interested."

"Are you kidding?" Stephanie asked. "How could you not be interested? Have you *seen* that guy's abs?"

"And his eyes," Leah jumped in.

"Yeah," Stephanie agreed. "And next to Luke, he's like the most popular guy in school."

Kristen saw a satisfied smile pass over Tracy's mouth. Luke Davis—sexy senior, starting quarterback, and all-around stud—was her boyfriend.

"I'd date Trevor in a second," Leah said.

"Anyone would," Tracy said. "Except for the one person he happens to be interested in." She slowly turned her gaze to Kristen, and Leah and Stephanie followed suit.

Kristen groaned. "Look, I already told you: *I'm. Not. Interested.* What do you want me to do?"

"I want you to give him a chance," Tracy said.

"Why?" Kristen asked. "Why do you care?"

"Because it would mean a lot to Luke—Trevor is his best friend, and from what Luke says, he really likes you."

---

jutted: stuck or projected   **indignantly:** resentfully or angrily   **aloof:** indifferent

Kristen found it hard to believe that Luke cared one way or another what happened—or didn't happen—between her and Trevor. Stephanie and Leah, however, were both nodding in agreement—Leah halfheartedly, due to her own interest in Trevor, but nodding nonetheless. She, like everyone else at Adams High, knew better than to **contradict** Tracy, who **wielded** her popularity like a battle-ax.

"He really does like you, you know," Stephanie confirmed. "He was totally heartbroken when he found out you weren't at my party. It was so cute."

"I bet," Kristen said. She sneaked a quick glance at Leah, who mouthed, *I told you so.* "But let me ask you something—was he so heartbroken that he left the party alone?"

"No-o," Stephanie answered. "He hooked up with Jen Pratt. But he waited until like 2 A.M., just in case you showed. And he made sure Jen knew it was just a one-night deal—it didn't mean anything."

"How romantic," Kristen sneered. She shot Leah a **smug** look and mouthed, *I told you so,* but Leah just shrugged.

"Don't be so **immature**, Kristen," Tracy said. "Jen was just a distraction. Trevor never would have even looked at anyone else if you'd been there. But you weren't, which reminds me — you blew us off. Where were you?"

For the second time that morning, Kristen felt her stomach tighten with **apprehension**. She hated having to **explicate** her every move to her friends—they were so **judgmental**. Still, the best thing to do was to just tell them and get it over with.

"I went to my dad's," Kristen said. She hoped they would let it go at that. All of *their* families were still nice and **intact**, and they weren't too **sympathetic** or understanding about how hard it had been for her since her parents' divorce a year ago. How nothing ever

---

contradict: oppose or challenge	**immature:** childish	**intact:** whole or complete
wielded: used	**apprehension:** dread or uneasiness	**sympathetic:** concerned or interested
smug: self-satisfied or conceited	**explicate:** explain	
	judgmental: critical	

felt okay anymore, and how impossible it was to care about the stuff she used to.

"I thought you were supposed to stay at your mom's this weekend," Leah said.

"I was, but she wasn't around, because of her new job. . . ."

"That's right, I saw her on the news last night," Stephanie said. "She was really good. Your mom is so pretty—and she looks so young."

Kristen cringed. Her mom *was* pretty, but Kristen was sick of hearing about it—from her friends, from her mom's friends, and especially from her mom's new **beau**, Dave, who also happened to be her coanchor on the weekend news. "Thanks," she said, struggling to maintain her **equanimity**. "So anyway . . . my dad called to see if I wanted to go to dinner, and I figured that would be better than the grilled cheese I was going to make, so I went. By the time we got out of the restaurant, it was already nine o'clock, and I could tell he didn't feel like driving me all the way home, so I just stayed at his house."

Her friends nodded. They seemed to be accepting her excuse at face value, which was good. She'd been afraid one of them—Leah in particular—would point out the fact that her father lived near the Reach, New Hampshire's **premier** surf spot, which of course had been a **factor** in Kristen's decision. Staying at his house had given Kristen a chance to hit the waves Sunday morning before returning to her mother's home in town, but thankfully none of her friends had picked up on that part of the equation.

For some reason, they all thought surfing was lame. Maybe she was just on the wrong coast or something. To them, it was a sport on **par** with mudding, or, as the locals called it, "muddin'." Muddin' involved driving a beat-up truck or jeep or SUV—whatever four-wheel-drive vehicle you could get your hands on—through fields and pits and wooded dirt roads until it was covered with mud. It was

---

beau: boyfriend
equanimity: composure

premier: foremost
factor: consideration

par: equal

the pastime of choice for many of the kids from rural areas—mostly students on the vocational track, and certainly not anyone worth Tracy Parks's attention.

None of Kristen's friends got her **preoccupation** with boards and wax, wet suits, and waves. Somehow, the concept of spending two hours at a time in forty-degree water **encased** in a full wet suit just to ride a few waves was one that didn't go over well in Kristen's peer group. They didn't understand what she found so **enthralling** about it, and they certainly didn't understand why she would **prefer** the **solitude** of the cold ocean to their company.

When it came down to it, they didn't understand much about Kristen these days—her **ardor** for surfing, her feelings about her parents' divorce, her **repugnance** for guys who acted like complete asses. But they'd been her friends since grade school, and that definitely counted for something. The four of them had **endured** a lot together, and Kristen still felt some **fidelity** to them, even if they didn't see eye to eye on much now.

"Okay, look," Tracy said. "Luke's having a party this weekend—on Friday night. His parents are leaving for Aruba on Thursday, so he's got the house to himself all weekend, and he's already found someone who can get a keg."

"Cool," Stephanie said.

"Sounds like fun," Leah agreed.

Tracy waited for Kristen to speak up, but Kristen simply held her gaze. Was she the only one who realized how lame it was to get all excited about getting *drunk*?

"Anyway," Tracy continued after a moment, "Trevor's going to be there, and I want you to be there too."

Kristen **resisted** the urge to roll her eyes. "Tracy, I—"

"Just give him a chance, Kristen. You two would make a really cute couple—wouldn't they?" Leah and Stephanie nodded like **obedient** puppies. "Hang out with him at Luke's on Friday night. Talk

preoccupation: interest or concern	**solitude:** seclusion or emptiness	**fidelity:** loyalty
encased: enclosed	**ardor:** passion	**resisted:** rejected or declined
enthralling: captivating	**repugnance:** dislike or distaste	**obedient:** docile or submissive
prefer: favor	**endured:** survived	

to him, get to know him better—really give him a chance. And then, if you're still not interested, I'll drop it. Okay?"

Kristen swallowed her protest and glanced toward Leah, who raised her eyebrows, her expression **imploring**.

"You promise you'll drop it?" Kristen asked, turning back to Tracy.

Tracy tucked her long brown hair behind her ear and smiled. "Promise," she said.

Kristen exhaled, slouching forward slightly. "All right. Fine. I'll go to the party, and I'll talk to Trevor."

"Thanks," Tracy said. "Luke will be really psyched." She turned to Stephanie. "Are you ready for precalc?"

"Mm-hmm," Stephanie said. "See you two in French."

"See you later," Leah said. Kristen just nodded. She hefted her backpack up on her shoulder, readjusting its weight, and **commenced** down the hall in the other direction with Leah, toward their first-period class—American history.

"I still don't get why Tracy suddenly cares so much who I date," Kristen muttered.

"Well, it might have something to do with what happened Saturday night," Leah said. She shot Kristen a **cryptic** look.

"Why? What happened?"

"Oh, nothing," Leah said with a smirk. "Except that Luke told Trevor—and everyone else at the party—that he thought you were hot."

Kristen stopped dead. "He *what*?"

"Well, he didn't mean to tell everyone, exactly. He was talking to Trevor in the living room, and the music was playing pretty loud, but then Angela Clark bumped into the stereo and switched the power off just as Luke was saying, 'Yeah, man, I'd go for Kristen Carmichael—she's hot.'"

"Oh my God, you're kidding," Kristen breathed.

---

imploring: pleading or begging

commenced: started

cryptic: inscrutable or mysterious

"Nope," Leah smiled. "Tracy was ripped. She barely spoke to him the rest of the night. *So-oo* . . . I guess she wants you to get a boyfriend—fast."

"But why Trevor?"

"Because he's already into you, he's popular, he's part of our group—*and* he's Luke's best friend."

"What does that have to do with it?"

"Isn't it obvious? If you date Trevor, you'll be off limits to Luke for good, even if things between you and Trevor don't work out. Guys are like that—they don't want their buddies' leftovers."

"Oh, that's nice. So Tracy wants me to be one of Trevor's leftovers," Kristen said. The politics of popularity were so **reprehensible**.

"I'm sure that's not her only motivation," Leah said. "She is your friend, you know."

"Lately, I'm not so sure," Kristen said.

"Well, she is," Leah insisted. "I admit, Tracy can be kind of . . . *superficial* at times—"

"That's a nice way to put it."

"But she really is a good person. She's probably hoping that dating Trevor will pull you back into the loop a little bit too."

"What do you mean?"

Leah cocked her head and looked Kristen in the eye. "You haven't exactly been spending a lot of time with us lately, you know. And even when you do, it's sort of like—I don't know—like your mind is somewhere else."

Kristen squinted, pretending to be **bewildered**, even though she knew exactly what Leah was talking about.

"Sometimes it even feels like you don't really want to hang around with us."

---

reprehensible: blameworthy   **superficial:** shallow   **bewildered:** puzzled
or displeasing

"Come on, you know that's not true," Kristen protested. "You guys are my best friends. Of course I want to hang around with you." But even as she said it, she knew it was a **fabrication**.

The thing was, she really *hadn't* enjoyed being around Leah, Tracy, and Stephanie much lately. She didn't care who was dating whom, and she wasn't interested in shopping at the mall or putting on makeup and doing her hair. She didn't even care about meeting guys—none of the guys at Adams High interested her. They all seemed **juvenile** and boring, and they all did the same loser thing on the weekend: drink.

"Well, I know that, but still, it would be nice to have you around more, and maybe if you and Trevor got together, you would be."

"I don't think there's much of a chance that—"

"Just give it a try," Leah said. "Maybe Tracy's right—maybe you two would make a really good couple. And besides, you don't want to get on Tracy's bad side."

"That's true," Kristen said. Tracy had a way of making life difficult for people she didn't get along with, and Kristen had a feeling that she was close to being one of those people. If Tracy thought for a second that Kristen was interested in Luke, she wouldn't hesitate to make Kristen's life hell. *So I'll go to the party and I'll talk to Trevor,* Kristen thought. Maybe it wouldn't be that bad. But even if it was, she'd be at her dad's this weekend, which meant surfing, and nothing could **blight** that.

---

fabrication: lie   juvenile: childish   blight: mar or taint

"Kristen? Do you have an answer for us?"

At the sound of her name, Kristen straightened up, blinking her way out of a daydream in which she'd been riding the crest of a fifteen-foot wave at the Reach. Ms. Fairfield, who taught eleventh-grade English and got way too **titillated** by *Macbeth*, placed her hands on her hips and waited.

"Well? What do you think, Kristen? Why does Lady Macbeth say, 'Out, damned spot!' in act five, scene one?"

I should know this, Kristen thought, although once again she'd **neglected** to do the reading for class. Still, it was such a famous line, she was sure she must have **encountered** it in a game of Trivial Pursuit at some point in her life. She **racked** her brain, but nothing came.

"Kristen?" Ms. Fairfield prodded, the slightest trace of a smile playing across her thin lips. She always seemed to take such pleasure in **embarrassing** students who'd been caught allowing their minds to wander from the **scintillating** topic of British literature. Kristen clenched her jaw **defiantly** and stared directly into her teacher's eyes.

"Was it because her dog peed on the carpet?" she asked without batting a lash. The entire class seemed to stiffen collectively, an **undercurrent** of deep breaths sweeping across the room. **Simultaneously**, the smug grin disappeared from Ms. Fairfield's face and was replaced by a thin, tight line. "Very amusing, Ms. Carmichael," she said dryly. "I'll see you after class." Then she called on Trevor Wilson, who correctly answered that Lady Macbeth, consumed with guilt, was referring to what she **perceived** to be bloodstains on

titillated: excited	**embarrassing:** humiliating or shaming	**undercurrent:** trace or sense
neglected: disregarded or forgotten	**scintillating:** stimulating or brilliant	**simultaneously:** concurrently
encountered: met or seen	**defiantly:** challengingly or boldly	**perceived:** saw
racked: afflicted or tormented		

her hands that she couldn't wash away, no matter how **diligently** she tried.

After he'd answered and Ms. Fairfield had turned to write something about **symbolism** on the board, Trevor leaned toward Kristen and whispered with a smirk, "*Or . . . she could have meant the dog.*"

Kristen couldn't help letting out a short laugh, causing Ms. Fairfield to stop writing and **momentarily** flash her a glare. Oh, well. The way Kristen saw it, if some **sadistic** teacher was bent on dishing out **humiliation**, she ought to be prepared to get a little back.

The rest of the class passed **uneventfully** with a **riveting** lecture on the layout of seventeenth-century Scottish castles. It was a yawn and a half, but Kristen kept herself awake by pretending to take notes while actually sketching surfboard decals. There was one in particular—with an orchid in a flame—that she thought she might actually take in to Rip Tide, the local surf shop, to see if she could get it **reproduced** as a decal. Her current board, a 9' 6" Hap Jacobs noserider that her uncle Pete had given to her just before he moved to Costa Rica, was a beautiful cranberry color with yellow trim, but it could use a little extra decoration. Kristen was just putting the finishing touches on it when the bell rang. Everyone rose from their seats at once, scrambling for the door. Kristen was about to join them when she was **summoned** back.

"Ms. Carmichael? I believe I asked you to stay," Ms. Fairfield called. Kristen's shoulders slumped forward slightly, but she managed not to groan. As her friends exited the room, she turned and trudged up to her teacher's desk, where Ms. Fairfield sat, writing quickly. She considered apologizing for the dog comment up front and just getting it over with but decided it was best to avoid admitting guilt unless it was absolutely necessary.

"I assume you know why I asked you to see me, Kristen," Ms. Fairfield said, fingering the **gaudy** gold Irish setter brooch that held

---

diligently: carefully
symbolism: system of representations
momentarily: instantly
sadistic: cruel

humiliation: shame or embarrassment
uneventfully: calmly or placidly
riveting: fascinating

reproduced: duplicated
summoned: called
gaudy: flashy or tasteless

her dark, fringed scarf together at the neck. She gazed down her nose at Kristen through the lenses of her black-rimmed glasses.

"I guess so," Kristen said with a half shrug. She wasn't volunteering anything. If Ms. Fairfield wanted to **castigate** her, she was going to have to do it on her own.

"**Flippant** remarks concerning urinating dogs during class time are not appreciated," Ms. Fairfield informed her, still fondling the brooch. "But that's not the only reason I wanted to talk with you."

"It's not?" Kristen asked, wrinkling her nose. What else could she have done?

"No. Actually, I wanted to speak to you about your performance in class this quarter, as well. It's nearly progress report time, and you're one of the students I have listed as 'in danger of failing.'"

Kristen drew back, her heart speeding up. "In danger of failing?" she echoed, trying to keep her voice even.

Ms. Fairfield nodded. "Yes, I'm afraid you are. Your quiz grades—specifically on *Macbeth*—have been **abysmal**."

Abysmal, Kristen thought. *Sheesh*. Ms. Fairfield was such a drama queen. If only she had a life outside of school, then maybe she'd stop turning every minor **incident** into a major **catastrophe**.

"From your answer in class today," Ms. Fairfield went on, "I assume you weren't able to complete last night's reading assignment. And looking back at your past quiz grades—a sixty-five, a seventy-two and a fifty-four—I find myself wondering if you've completed *any* of the assigned reading for this quarter," she added, the self-satisfied, **malicious** smirk reappearing. "Have you?"

"Well," Kristen started. "I am a little behind, but—"

"Kristen, we read acts one and two aloud in class, and I went over them in detail, yet you still managed to fail the quiz. Are you having difficulty understanding the material?"

"No, I just—"

---

castigate: punish
flippant: frivolous or impertinent

abysmal: awful
incident: disturbance or confrontation

catastrophe: calamity or misfortune
malicious: spiteful

"What is it then? Are you simply not paying attention at all?" Ms. Fairfield asked.

Ouch. But really, how could her teacher expect her to care so much about her **tedious, monotonous** class, when all these huge things were happening in her life? "Well, I guess maybe I do find it a little hard," she ventured, hoping her teacher would buy it.

"I see," Ms. Fairfield said, nodding. "Well, then, the detention I'm giving you for **inappropriate** behavior could be just what the doctor ordered. You can sit here and do your reading, and if you have any questions, I'll be right here to answer them."

"You're giving me a detention?"

"Yes," Ms. Fairfield answered, handing Kristen a disciplinary form on which she'd already filled in Kristen's name, the date, and the phrase "inappropriate comments in class." There was a place at the bottom for one of Kristen's parents to sign, confirming that they'd read it. "I'll see you this afternoon at one forty-five sharp."

"Wait—you want me to stay *today*?" Kristen asked. Again, Ms. Fairfield nodded. "But I can't," Kristen told her. "I won't have a ride home. My parents will both be at work. I'll have to take the bus."

"You can take the late bus. It leaves at four-thirty."

"Four-thirty?" Kristen repeated. "But that's like two and a half hours. How long is my detention?"

"Two and a half hours," Ms. Fairfield said. "So it should work out perfectly."

Kristen's jaw dropped. Most teachers gave shorter detentions—a half hour, tops—because they didn't want to hang out at school any later than they had to. But apparently Ms. Fairfield didn't mind the extra time, a detail that Kristen took as further evidence that her teacher's life **consisted** of school, school and school. Her idea of getting wild and crazy was probably showing up five minutes late for a faculty meeting.

---

tedious: exhausting or uninteresting

monotonous: boring
inappropriate: unsuitable

consisted: comprised

"Here—you'll need this," Ms. Fairfield said, handing Kristen a pink piece of paper. It was a late pass so that she wouldn't get in trouble for arriving at her next class after the bell.

"Thanks," Kristen said automatically, realizing **instantaneously** that thanking Ms. Fairfield for a late pass after having received a two-and-a-half-hour detention was **akin** to thanking a police officer for a speeding ticket. Unfortunately, the thought came to her after the words had already left her mouth. She stood for a minute, chewing the inside of her cheek and thinking, but as she was unable to come up with any way of taking her **gratitude** back, she decided her best course of action was just to leave.

"I'll see you at one forty-five," Ms. Fairfield called as Kristen walked out, but Kristen didn't bother to answer. Saying thanks had been bad enough. She didn't need to add to it by exchanging pleasant good-byes.

*   *   *   *   *

Five hours later, Kristen swung open the front door to her mother's apartment and immediately wished she were back in detention. *Macbeth* and Ms. Fairfield would have been a welcome sight in **contrast** to the scene before her. Hannah Graham, weekend anchor for KJKF, was locked in a kiss with her coanchor, Dave Goodall, on the sofa. Her shirt was rumpled and her clothing was **disheveled**.

Of course, the image only lasted a split second, because the moment Ms. Graham heard the door slam shut, she leapt onto her own cushion and slipped immediately into her television voice.

"Kristen, honey . . . I didn't hear you come in," she said, **enunciating** far too clearly. Dave, who was in the process of straightening and rebuttoning his shirt, waved awkwardly. Kristen just stared. "He and I were just . . ." Ms. Graham paused to clear her throat. "Well, we didn't realize you'd be coming in just then," she finished with an

---

instantaneously: immediately
akin: similar

gratitude: thankfulness or appreciation
contrast: comparison

disheveled: ruffled or disordered
enunciating: speaking or articulating

overly **enthusiastic** smile. Kristen curled her lip in disgust. Her mother's short blond hair was a mess, and her lipstick was smudged. "Sorry to show up and ruin everything, Dave," she said.

"Um, I, uh . . . ," Dave stammered. He blinked rapidly and turned to Kristen's mother for help. Unfortunately, she was **preoccupied** with fixing her hair.

"Kristen Graham Carmichael—that was uncalled for and completely inappropriate."

"Huh. Must be something in the air," Kristen said. She tossed the detention notice Ms. Fairfield had given her onto the coffee table as she walked by.

"What's this?" her mother asked, snatching it up. Kristen kept walking, heading straight for her room. "Kristen?" her mother called. "Did you have a detention this afternoon?"

"Yeah, good thing, huh?" Kristen said over her shoulder. "If I'd gotten home on time, I can't even imagine what I would have **interrupted**!"

"Kristen!" her mother **chastised**, but Kristen didn't stop. She went into her room, closed her door, put on a Jack Johnson CD, turned the volume to ten, and tried to shove the image of her mother making out with Dave on the living room sofa out of her mind.

---

enthusiastic: excited or eager
preoccupied: engrossed or distracted

interrupted: disturbed or disrupted

chastised: scolded or rebuked

"Are you sure you can't come?" Leah asked, glancing over at Kristen as they walked out of school the next day. "Just for an hour or so?"

Kristen had no desire whatsoever to accompany Leah, Tracy and Stephanie on a shopping trip to the mall. Buying a new top for Luke's party wasn't exactly one of her top **priorities** for the afternoon. Surfing, on the other hand, was.

She'd had a chance to check the closest weather buoy information online during a quick trip to the computer lab in study hall, and it sounded like the swell was decent out at the Reach. "I would," Kristen said, "but my dad's picking me up, and he'll want to head straight back."

"I could give you a ride home."

"That's like forty-five minutes out of your way, Leah."

"I don't mind."

Well I do, Kristen thought. "Thanks," she said, "but he's already on his way, and he'd be annoyed if he drove all the way into town just to hear that I wanted to go to the mall."

"So call him," Leah said, producing her cell phone. "Save him the trip. He can turn around wherever he is, and I'll drive you to Perkins Beach when we're done at the mall." She flashed a hopeful smile that made it even more **complicated** for Kristen to **refuse**. She hated to **disappoint** her friend, but she needed to be by herself. She needed the ocean. The thought of being out there riding the waves made every inch of her skin itch to just get there already.

"Well—," Kristen started, feeling torn. Then she saw a black BMW turn down the school drive. "Oh—there he is," she said, doing her best to sound **despondent**.

---

priorities: preferences
complicated: complex or involved

refuse: decline
disappoint: frustrate

despondent: desperate or hopeless

Leah turned just in time to see Mr. Carmichael pull up to the curb. "Hi, Leah," he called as he lowered the automatic window on the passenger side.

"Hi, Mr. Carmichael."

"How's basketball going?"

Leah shot a quick glance at Kristen. "Actually, I'm not playing this year," she said.

"Oh, that's too bad," Mr. Carmichael said. "You were always so good. I remember watching you bring the ball all the way down the court and score the winning basket in that game against . . . " He paused to scratch his balding head. "Which team was that?"

"Franklin," Leah said. **Benevolently**, she didn't embarrass him by adding the words *middle school*. She'd tried out for the Adams High team freshman year, gotten cut after two weeks, and never tried out again. The game Mr. Carmichael was **referring** to had been one of Leah's last—back in eighth grade. She shot another raised-eyebrow look at Kristen, this time with a smirk.

"I better get going," Kristen said, turning to face Leah so that her back was to her father's car. They exchanged smiles, and Kristen remembered that they still had one thing in common—out-of-touch dads.

"Call me later," Leah said as Kristen opened the passenger side door.

"I will," Kristen said. And then, as her father pulled away, she added, "Have fun at the mall."

"Thanks!" Leah called, waving.

"What's going on at the mall?" Mr. Carmichael asked, heading toward the main road.

"Nothing," Kristen shrugged. "Leah's just going shopping with Tracy and Steph."

Mr. Carmichael came to a stop at the end of the road and gazed over at Kristen. "Did you want to go with them?" he asked.

---

benevolently: kindly   referring: alluding

Kristen shrugged. "No. Not really."

"Because if you do, I could always pick you up in another hour or so."

"I said *no*," Kristen snapped. Almost immediately she felt a stab of guilt, but she couldn't help feeling **frustrated**. Why didn't anyone ever listen to her anymore?

"I just thought I'd offer," Mr. Carmichael said. He turned left on Route 4 and headed toward the coast.

For a while, they traveled in silence, Kristen staring out her window, her father keeping his eyes on the road. It wasn't until they were nearly home, when Kristen spotted the surf shop quickly appearing in—and disappearing from—her view, that she finally spoke up.

"Hey, Dad—can we stop at Rip Tide? I need to pick up some wax." Her father applied the brakes and put on his left turn signal. "Thanks," Kristen said.

After a quick U-turn, Mr. Carmichael pulled into a vacant space across the road from Rip Tide, just in front of Café Olé, one of the newer coffee shops in town. It had opened a few months ago when one of the local **florists**, Flowers to Die For, had gone out of business. Given the name, no one—except the owners, who'd thought it was a catchy **appellation**—had been the least bit surprised that it had failed to **prosper**.

"I'll be right back," Kristen said, jumping out and slamming her door. An older man in a green pickup stopped to let her cross, and Kristen smiled and waved as she jogged in front of him.

In the store, she breezed past the clothing racks of surf couture that kept Rip Tide in business and headed straight for the counter. "Dr. Zog's, cold," she said, nodding toward the display hanging behind the cashier. There was no age limit for **purchasing** surfboard wax, but because of its name—and its **convenient** pocket-

---

frustrated: thwarted or obstructed
florists: flower merchants

appellation: designation or title
prosper: flourish

purchasing: acquiring
convenient: handy

size container—Dr. Zog's Sex Wax was the most shoplifted item Rip Tide carried, which was why you had to ask for it at the register.

"Good waves today," the guy behind the counter commented.

"Supposed to be," Kristen replied.

"They are," the clerk said. "I was out this morning. We're finally getting some of that swell that's been pounding Cape Cod. Should last for a few days, at least."

She looked at him more closely, realizing who he was. What was his name again? *Ken.* She'd heard his friends calling to him out at the Reach before when they were all getting ready to leave and he was still catching waves. The midwinter surf could be **bitterly** cold in New Hampshire, but it was also the time of year when the waves were the best. Due to the temperature, however, people rarely stayed out for more than an hour. Except for Ken. He always seemed to be able to last longer than anyone else. Because of that, Kristen had always considered him pretty hard-core. And cool.

"What kind of wet suit do you wear?" she asked, handing him the twenty her mother had given her for lunch money that week.

"Usually a Viper three-two. Need a bag?" he asked, holding up her wax.

"No, thanks," Kristen said. "A three-two, huh?"

"Yep. I usually wear a rash guard too."

"And that's it?"

Ken nodded. "That's it." Three-twos were pretty common. In fact, that was what Kristen wore too.

"So how do you manage to stay out so much longer than everyone else?"

Ken shrugged. "I don't know. **Stubborn** mind, strong will, and a decent amount of body fat, I guess," he said, gripping his midriff. "Course, if *you're* looking for a way to **maximize** your time in the water, Bodyline makes a four-three with a titanium lining. S'posed to be one of the warmest around."

---

bitterly: severely or unpleasantly   **stubborn:** unyielding   **maximize:** increase

"How much?"

"Five hundred."

Kristen winced. "That's a little out of my league right now."

"How 'bout a vest, then? Seventhwave makes a nice one with a bladder for around two hundred." Again Kristen grimaced at the price. "They make a hot top for about one-fifty," Ken suggested.

"Is there anything I could do for under, say . . . *thirty dollars?*" Kristen had already blown most of the cash she'd saved from her summer job as a cashier at the local grocery, so now she was relying on the **generosity** of her parents and whatever she could save of her weekly lunch money.

Ken scrunched his nose. "Hmm. Well, there are a few vests for a little over thirty that might help, but for *under* thirty you could pick up some of those hand or foot warmers that skiers and hunters use. I've never tried 'em myself, but Bobby—you know Bobby, tall red-head, always wears that blue-and-yellow suit?" Kristen nodded. There weren't a lot of surfers who went out on a regular basis in the winter, so they all pretty much knew each others' faces, even if they didn't exchange names or personal information. It was too cold for much more than a friendly nod.

"Yeah, well, Bobby told me he gets five or six of them on the coldest days and stuffs them right into his wetsuit before he goes out. Said it makes a big difference."

"Really?" Kristen asked. "Hmm. I'll have to try that."

"I ordered a case yesterday after he told me. They should be in by Thursday. Stop back in if you get a chance and I'll give you a deal. Then you can come back and tell me how they worked so I know if I should keep buying and **recommending** them or not."

"Deal," Kristen said, smiling. It wasn't the first time Ken had cut her a break on gear—he did it for all the local surfers from time to time. It was sort of like a discount card program without the discount card, and it didn't hurt his **revenue** at all. Most of his profit

---

generosity: open-handedness or charity

recommending: endorsing or promoting

revenue: income or profits

came from clothing sales, and the clothing was mostly purchased by nonsurfers who'd gotten hooked on surf culture while watching one of MTV's Spring Breaks or some other television show.

As Kristen got ready to leave, she held up the wax. "Thanks."

"Have a good ride," Ken replied, nodding.

Kristen jogged back across the street and hopped into her father's car, which was still running.

As he pulled out, executing another **exemplary** U-turn to put them back on track, he glanced over at her purchase. "Why do they call it *Sex* Wax, anyway?" he asked, eyeing the label.

Kristen groaned.

"What? I'm just wondering where it got its name. Do you know?"

"No."

"Do you care?" Mr. Carmichael asked.

"Not really."

Her father glanced over at her with narrowed eyes. "Well, this has been a lovely **conversation**, Kristen. Perhaps we can continue it over dinner."

Kristen sighed. If her father wanted good conversation, he should come up with more intelligent topics. And recognize the fact that three years had passed since the last time Leah had played basketball.

"What *is* dinner, anyway?" Kristen asked. For the first six months she'd spent nights or weekends at her father's, they'd **subsisted** on pizza, takeout, and TV dinners. Over the last few months, though, he'd managed to cut back on the convenience food and actually started to cook.

"Salmon. With rosemary, rice, salad, and Carrie."

"Curry?"

"No—*Carrie*. As in Sandborn. She's coming over for dinner tonight."

---

exemplary: excellent   conversation: discussion   subsisted: existed

"Again?" Kristen asked. Her father's girlfriend, who also happened to be his secretary—or, *ahem*, administrative assistant, as Carrie would insist—had started joining them for dinner on a semi-regular basis over the last few weeks. Kristen knew her father was trying to get them to bond, but instead of growing closer to Carrie during shared meals, Kristen had learned to dread her visits. Carrie was always **beleaguering** Kristen with questions about school, boys, friends, parties, and surfing—all topics about which she seemed completely clueless.

Ironically, at twenty years younger than Mr. Carmichael, Carrie was closer to Kristen's age than to his, but she still seemed even more out of it than Kristen's **ultraconservative** father, if that was even possible.

"Yes, *again*," Mr. Carmichael said. "And I'd appreciate it if you'd try to at least exchange a few words with her. She's trying very hard to get to know you, and—"

"Why does she need to know *me*? She's *your* girlfriend," Kristen said.

Mr. Carmichael took a deep breath and let it out slowly, the way he did every time he was starting to get upset. It drove Kristen crazy. "Yes, she is my girlfriend, and she's very important to me, as are you. I just think it would be nice if the two people I care about most could get along."

"They do," Kristen muttered under her breath. The two people he cared about most were himself and Carrie, and they seemed to be getting along just fine.

"Excuse me?" Mr. Carmichael asked as he pulled into his drive and pushed a button on the garage door opener.

"Nothing," Kristen said. There was no point in repeating it. If she did, her father would just do his breathing thing again to call attention to how upset she was making him and how well he was controlling it. "I'm gonna go surfing. What time is dinner?"

---

beleaguering: harassing   **ultraconservative:** extremely traditional

"Dinner is at six sharp, but Carrie is coming at five and I'd like you to be here."

Kristen glanced at the clock on her father's dashboard. *"Five?* That's only like an hour and a half. I'll barely be in the water and I'll have to get out again. Why do I have to come back so early?"

"Number one, because it's still getting dark at five, and I don't want you surfing when the light is going down. And number two, because I'm telling you to," Mr. Carmichael said. He gazed at Kristen for a moment, his deep brown eyes—the ones she'd **inherited** from him—serious, his forehead creased. Kristen blinked and looked away, gathering her backpack and her wax as her father reached into the backseat for his briefcase.

"Fine," Kristen said. "I'll be back at five." She opened her car door and walked into the house and straight to her room without so much as glancing in her father's direction again. Then she stripped off her jeans and T-shirt, replacing them with her rash guard, neoprene shorts, and GUL three-two, grabbed her surfboard from its resting spot in the corner of her closet, and headed for the beach. Her father's house was just across the street from the beach entrance, and there was a path through the dunes that led straight to the Reach, so Kristen was able to get there on foot in less than ten minutes.

As soon as she came over the **knoll** that hid the ocean from view, Kristen could see that the waves were pounding. The New Hampshire coast was **definitely** getting the swell that had hit Cape Cod late last week, just like Ken had said. And it was solid surf—about four feet high and glassy. There was no wind **disturbing** the lines.

Kristen felt the corners of her mouth curving upward as she took in the waves, noting that cold-weather smiles seemed to require more effort than warm-weather ones. Not only that, but they felt as though they **etched** more **permanent** wrinkles in the face—features that Kristen would one day refer to as "surf lines."

---

inherited: derived   definitely: surely   etched: carved
knoll: mound   disturbing: upsetting   permanent: everlasting

Not wanting to waste a moment, she tromped straight down to the shore, snow crunching under her boots until she reached the tide line. She propped her surfboard gently against a smooth rock and took a seat, swapping her Gore-Tex L.L. Bean hikers for the five-millimeter split-toe booties she'd picked up at Rip Tide last season. Next, she pulled her newly **acquired** tub of Dr. Zog's from her black gear bag and waxed down her board. When that was done, she roughed it up with a comb for better **traction**, traded her knit cap for a cold-water hood, slipped on her SLX gloves and bounded into the water.

In less than thirty seconds, Kristen was in far enough to start paddling out. She jumped onto her board, positioning herself on her stomach so that her toes were just touching the back edge of her board, and began paddling furiously with her arms. With no time to spare, she needed to get out to the sandbar where the waves broke as fast as she could.

Luckily, there was no one else out this afternoon, so she didn't have to worry about getting into a lineup or waiting her turn for a wave. Most of the locals were probably still at work, and they **typically** hit the beach in the early morning as opposed to late afternoon, anyway.

After about ten minutes, Kristen had nearly reached the break, and she saw a set coming in that looked particularly promising. She let the first wave go by, holding tight to her board, and then began paddling like crazy into the next one. At first it appeared to be a three-footer—about waist high—but as Kristen got closer, she realized that it was actually nearer to four or five feet. It wasn't an overheader, but considering that Kristen herself was only 5' 5", it came in somewhere near shoulder height.

As the wave approached, Kristen forced any **irrelevant** thoughts out of her head and focused solely on her board, the water, and the present moment. When she felt the nose of her board beginning to

---

acquired: obtained   **typically:** normally   **irrelevant:** inappropriate or
traction: friction or drag   inapplicable

lift, she stopped paddling and gripped the sides of her board tightly with both hands. Then, careful to keep her weight centered, she pushed herself up—hopping to bring both legs forward and **transitioning** onto her feet.

As the wave crested, Kristen's board turned slightly. She leaned into the turn with her hips, forcing her board toward the lip, where she was able to ride for a few seconds before dropping down the face of the wave and finding a solid spot on the shoulder. Already she'd been up for nearly twenty seconds, which was a pretty solid ride, but the wave was still strong, and as long as she didn't fall, it looked like Kristen might be able to ride it most of the way in.

With her right leg in front, Kristen **crouched** low and got ready to attempt a cross-step. It was a move she'd been working on for a while, hoping to one day make it to the front of her board, where she could then hang five or ten off the edge. Noseriding, her Uncle Pete had always said, was the one riding **technique** that truly separated longboarders from shortboarders. It was a move that couldn't be executed on a shortboard, and, according to Pete, there was nothing in the world like it.

Pete was Kristen's mom's younger brother, and he was Kristen's favorite uncle by far. Her father had a few brothers, but they lived in Arizona, and Kristen hadn't seen or heard from them for years. Pete, on the other hand, sent postcards to Kristen and her mom every other month or so, and he was always inviting Kristen out to visit him in Costa Rica, where he said the surfing was unbelievable.

Kristen wished she could go, but she didn't have the money for a plane ticket and neither of her parents had seemed up for springing for one. Her mom had agreed that they should go visit on more than one **occasion**, but something always **precluded** her from making any concrete plans—her demanding work schedule, her recent promotion . . . *Dave.*

---

transitioning: progressing or changing
crouched: bent

technique: style or method
occasion: time or instance

precluded: stopped or prohibited

The last time Kristen had mentioned Costa Rica to her mother, her mom had **insinuated** that if she went, she'd want Dave to come along. That **proviso** had been enough to get Kristen to drop the subject **permanently**. She wasn't exactly up for a vacation with her mom's boyfriend. Although it wouldn't really have mattered too much who was around because Kristen would be hanging out with Pete all the time anyway.

Back before Pete had joined the Peace Corps and moved away, he used to take Kristen out surfing on a regular basis—at least once or twice a week. In fact, he was the one who'd taught her to surf four years ago, when she was only twelve, and gotten her completely hooked on the sport. But it was after her parents divorced and Pete moved away that surfing became more than just a hobby. It was like she *needed* it—nothing made sense anywhere else, but out here she was totally free.

Kristen crossed her left leg in front of her right, keeping both knees bent and her center of gravity low. Eventually, she managed to plant her left foot solidly on the board so that her weight was evenly **distributed** again, and then she repeated the process with her right leg. After two completed steps she nearly lost her balance, but by sinking even lower on her board and pressing all her weight into her toes and heels, she was able to **regain** it.

When she was steady again, her eyes darted toward the front of her board. *Two more steps and I'll be on the nose,* she thought. If she made it, she'd have to write Pete and let him know—he'd be stoked. With that thought in mind, Kristen got ready to move her left leg again, but before she'd even raised her heel, her board started to tilt so that the right rail was almost completely underwater, and she had to **abandon** the cross-step to readjust again.

Now, after a nearly thirty-second ride, Kristen knew she didn't have much longer before the wave broke altogether, so she cross-stepped back to her original **position** and turned her nose into the

---

insinuated: hinted
proviso: stipulation or condition

permanently: eternally
distributed: apportioned
regain: recover

abandon: reject or forsake
position: location

wave, attempting to climb closer to the lip and increase her speed. Unfortunately, she misjudged and turned too far, causing her nose to **pearl**, which slowed her down **dramatically** and pitched her off the front of the board.

She felt her leash jerk at her ankle as she went under, and she tried to **estimate** the **approximate** position of her board so she could avoid ramming her head into it when she resurfaced. As the wave broke, it held her under for a good ten seconds or so—not a long time by any measure, but still, in forty-degree water it was **significant**. By the time she came up, Kristen's lungs felt like they were empty and **collapsing** in on themselves. She gasped **involuntarily**, taking in a huge amount of air, which was both refreshing and painful at the same time. But despite the sting at the back of her throat, Kristen was **elated**. She'd ridden that wave for close to forty seconds, which made it one of the longest rides she'd ever done. And she'd been two steps short of the nose—maybe even just one—which was definitely the closest she'd ever gotten. She hadn't been able to hang ten, or even five, but she might just have to write to Pete anyway.

Kristen treaded water for a moment, turning to locate and recover her board, which, thanks to the leash, was floating nearby. She placed both hands on the side and got ready to kick up onto it, but as she **extended** her legs, she realized that she could touch bottom. In fact, when she stood, the water was below her shoulders. Whirling toward the shore, Kristen discovered that she was only about twenty-five feet from the rock where she'd left her stuff.

"Whoa," she breathed. *That was one hell of a ride.* It had brought her almost all the way back to shore. Kristen turned toward the break again and **surveyed** the swell. It was still going strong, and if she moved quickly, she could probably catch one more wave before it was time to head back to her father's house. For dinner with Carrie. *Ugh.* That thought alone made Kristen shiver. So, putting it

pearl: dive into the water (not an SAT word)	**approximate**: rough	**elated**: ecstatic
dramatically: incredibly	**significant**: meaningful	**extended**: stretched
estimate: calculate	**collapsing**: disintegrating	**surveyed**: observed or evaluated
	involuntarily: instinctively	

quickly out of her mind, she pulled herself back onto her board and started paddling out again.

There was no way she could hope to catch another wave as easily as she'd caught the first one or to ride it half as well, but still, as she headed toward the break, Kristen felt a certain sense of **tranquility** settle over her. She was **exhilarated** but calm; **invigorated** yet relaxed. It was the Zen of surfing, and it was what she loved most.

Out there in the ocean, she felt at home like she did in no other place. The salt air **nurtured** her soul while the waves **challenged** her will. In the **vastness** of the ocean, she could see how **insignificant** and **trivial** most of the rituals of daily life truly were, and when she stood on her board and **navigated** her way along the waves, she felt like she was part of something bigger than homework and high school. Although the ocean was raw and **merciless**, it didn't lie and it didn't leave, and you couldn't tackle it half-heartedly or fake your way through it. There was nothing superficial about it—**contrary** to everyone and everything else in Kristen's life.

As she paddled out, Kristen focused on the distant horizon. She was able to gain a clear **perspective** of it every time the outer edge of a wave bounced her upward. It was indeed beginning to get dark already, and although the days were getting longer now, for the next month or so sunset would remain within the five o'clock hour. Still, even in the **dissipating** light, the sea was beautiful. Kristen sighed, wishing she could drift forever in the cool Atlantic, where everything was pure and **tranquil** and real. But she knew she couldn't, even if she gave herself over to the ocean completely. That was the one problem with waves: sooner or later, they always brought you back to shore.

*   *   *   *   *

tranquility: peacefulness
exhilarated: excited or stimulated
invigorated: fortified or refreshed
nurtured: strengthened or sustained

challenged: tested
vastness: enormity
insignificant: unimportant or inconsequential
trivial: banal
navigated: maneuvered or guided

merciless: pitiless
contrary: opposed
perspective: angle or viewpoint
dissipating: vanishing
tranquil: calm

By the time Kristen got back to her father's house, it was 5:05, and Carrie had already arrived. As she entered the mudroom **via** the garage, Kristen felt **nauseated** by the sound of Carrie and her father laughing in the kitchen.

"I think you need a little more flour on your hands," Carrie said in a voice that **resembled** the one most people reserved for babies and puppies.

Mr. Carmichael giggled. Actually *giggled*. "I think *you* need some flour on your nose," he replied. This comment was followed by the sound of a minor scuffle and more giggling from both of them.

"Steven!" Carrie squealed. "I can't believe you did that!"

"It looks cute."

Kristen **recoiled** as she heard the words come out of her father's mouth. If she'd eaten lunch that day, she probably would have lost it.

For a moment, she considered turning around and going back outside. However, as she was still wet and shivering from her surf session, going back into the thirty-degree air was not an **option**. Kristen needed a hot shower, a plush towel, some cozy sweats and a pair of wool socks, pronto, which, unfortunately, meant walking through the kitchen and watching her father and Carrie flirt like a couple of monkeys in heat.

She leaned her board against the wall with its tail solidly planted on one of the boot mats to catch any remaining drips and headed toward the sound of her father's **puerile** mating call—that high-pitched giggle. It really turned Kristen's stomach. Apparently Carrie went for men who laughed like little girls. She currently had Mr. Carmichael backed up against the counter near the stove, where she was attempting to dab his nose with flour and nibble on his neck. How sweet.

Kristen had almost managed to **circumvent** the whole scene without being spotted—or throwing up—when they both gasped.

---

via: through
nauseated: sickened, disgusted

resembled: was similar to
recoiled: flinched
option: choice

puerile: silly or childish
circumvent: evade or avoid

"Kristen!" her father boomed. "I didn't hear you come in." *Probably because your girlfriend's tongue was stuck in your ear,* Kristen thought, but she managed to keep it to herself.

"How was the surf?" Carrie asked, a **mawkish** grin stretching across her face. "Did you catch any waves?"

Kristen scowled. The way Carrie said it, "catching waves" sounded like something kindergarteners might do in gym class. "A couple," Kristen answered. "I didn't have a lot of time, though," she added, frowning at her father.

"Well, I'm glad you're back," Mr. Carmichael said, ignoring her look. "It's getting dark, and we're making pizza." Kristen glanced out the window. It *was* getting dark, but she could have surfed safely for another forty-five minutes if it hadn't been for dinner with Carrie. "Why don't you go change your clothes? Then you can come back and add your toppings," her father said in a positively **effervescent** tone. Kristen was beginning to feel as though she'd walked into a **perkiness immersion** program.

"Actually, I need to take a shower. Why don't you just go ahead and do mine?" Kristen said.

"We can wait," Carrie offered. "I'm not starving—are you, Steven?"

Mr. Carmichael shrugged. "Nope."

Carrie looked brightly at Kristen. "So go ahead and take your shower. Your dad and I can amuse each other until you're ready, and then we can all do our pizzas together."

Oh goody! Kristen thought. *And will Marcia, Jan, and Cindy help too? What about Greg, Peter, and Bobby?* Her lip curled involuntarily as she glared at her father. With Carrie around, he was like some kind of retro TV dad—all **solicitous** and involved. It was freaky. In the fifteen years that he had lived with Kristen and her mother, he hadn't helped with dinner or dabbed flour on anyone's nose once. And his voice had certainly never **effervesced**.

---

mawkish: insipid
effervescent: enthusiastic or lively

perkiness: cheeriness
immersion: dunking
solicitous: concerned

effervesced: enthused

"Go on—really," Carrie **persisted**. "It will be fun. And while we're making our pizzas, maybe you can answer a few questions about surfing for me." Kristen's stomach tightened and the glare she was giving her father **intensified**. "I was flipping through your *Longshore* magazine earlier—"

"Long*board*," Kristen muttered through clenched teeth.

"Oh—*Longboard*—that's right," Carrie said, chuckling at her mistake. "Anyway, there was an article on nose-surfing, and I—"

"It's nose*riding*," Kristen practically hissed, "and I need to shower or I'm going to freeze." Then, before Carrie could ask her about hanging eight or paddling down, she turned abruptly and left.

"Kristen," she heard her father call, the **stern** edge creeping back into his voice. But Kristen marched down the hall to her room and slammed the door. Why did she have to put up with this? Her mother making out in the living room, her father playing house with his Barbie-doll girlfriend—sometimes Kristen felt like she was the parent and they were her children.

She peeled off her wet suit and threw on the white terry-cloth bathrobe her mother had given her to keep at her father's house, pulling it tight around her body and **cinching** the sash. Then she flopped down on her bed and stared at the ceiling.

As she focused on the **imperfections** in the sheetrock above her, Kristen couldn't help wondering how much longer the ocean alone could **sustain** her.

---

persisted: continued
intensified: strengthened or sharpened

stern: serious or critical
cinching: tightening

imperfections: flaws or defects
sustain: support or reinforce

"Is that what you're wearing?" Leah **inquired** as she opened the door.

Kristen stood on her best friend's front porch and stared down at her outfit. Hiking boots, boot-leg jeans, and two long-sleeved henleys, layered—white under forest green. "Yeah. Why?"

Leah grabbed Kristen by the arm and pulled her inside. "First, lose the boots," she said. Kristen untied the laces and kicked her hikers onto the boot mat by the front door. "Now, come with me," Leah said, and once again she grabbed Kristen by the arm, leading the way upstairs and toward the back of the house, where her **overwhelmingly** pink bedroom was located. Kristen almost **gagged** as she walked in, so **pungent** was the scent of CK One.

"What have you been doing in here?" she asked with an **exaggerated** cough. "Training to be a Filene's perfume lady?"

Leah cocked her head. "Very funny," she said, "but no. Actually, instead of spraying the perfume directly onto my skin, I prefer to spray it around the room and then walk through it. That way I get a light mist all over—it lasts longer and it's not too strong."

Kristen listened with **incredulity**. These were the things in which her friends were interested. "Welcome to Perfume 101 with Leah McDonnell," she **jested**, speaking into a hairbrush she'd found on Leah's desk.

"What you need is Fashion 101," Leah said, eyeing Kristen's clothes once again. "I can't believe you actually *chose* this outfit."

"What's wrong with what I'm wearing?"

"Nothing—if you're planning to spend the night shoveling driveways," Leah replied. "But I thought you were going to a party."

Kristen shrugged. "I am."

---

inquired: asked or queried
overwhelmingly: shockingly or staggeringly
gagged: choked or retched
pungent: sharp or acrid
exaggerated: overplayed or inflated
incredulity: disbelief
jested: joked

"Well, then, let's get you dressed for it." Leah dove into her closet and **emerged** with a couple of articles of clothing on hangers. "Try these," she said, offering them to Kristen.

Kristen took the clothes and eyed them **tentatively**. "I don't know, Leah. This isn't really my style." Leah dressed like someone out of an eighties movie. Currently she was wearing black pin-striped trousers, stiletto heels, and a tight, bright pink stretch blouse with a wide collar and three-quarter sleeves. She swore the eighties were in again, but Kristen wasn't sure.

"Neither is what you're wearing," Leah said. "I've seen you dress better for the dentist, Kristen. Honestly, it's like you're not even trying to look good."

"That's not true," Kristen **protested**. It wasn't that she wasn't try-ing—it was just that she didn't care. She wouldn't even be going to Luke's stupid party if Leah hadn't been **badgering** her about it all day.

"Come on, just try them on and see how they look," Leah said.

"Fine," Kristen replied with a sigh. "Give them to me." **Surren-dering** seemed the easiest route. She draped the clothes over Leah's wooden chair and shed her own so she could try them on. The outfit consisted of a stretchy leopard-print miniskirt that sat well below Kristen's belly button and barely covered her butt, paired with a tight black midriff-bearing tank top.

"Oh my God, you look *so* hot," Leah said when Kristen had them both on. "But you need **accessories**," she added, returning to the closet to **forage** some more.

Kristen stared at herself in the full-length mirror, **observing** how the clothes **revealed** the shape of her body, and **grimaced**. "I don't think so," she said. "I look like a hooker."

Leah stuck her head back out of the closet and scowled. "Not with those wool socks, you don't," she said. "But with *these* . . ." She grinned as she held up a pair of patent leather knee-high boots.

---

emerged: appeared
tentatively: uncertainly
protested: objected or complained

badgering: harassing or annoying
surrendering: relinquishing or yielding
accessories: extras

forage: rummage
observing: noticing or studying
revealed: exposed
grimaced: frowned

Kristen took one look at the heels and shook her head. "No way. When I started surfing and wearing flip-flops all summer, I promised myself I'd never cram my feet into any stupid pointy-toed girl shoes again—especially ones with three-inch heels. Trust me—I wouldn't even last an hour."

Leah stood with her hands on her hips, squinting and **scrutinizing** Kristen's **countenance**. After a moment, she either decided that Kristen was being sincere or that shoes weren't worth **squabbling** over, or maybe she just got an idea for another outfit. Whatever the reason, her frown disappeared and she headed back into the closet for a second try.

"What about these?" she asked, holding up a pair of wide-toed, loaferesque shoes with a chunky heel.

Kristen inhaled deeply. It wasn't exactly the kind of foot **apparel** she'd normally **opt** for, but something told her that her life would be a whole lot easier if she would just **endure** them. "I could wear those," she said.

Immediately, Leah's smile reappeared. "Great—we'll build your outfit from there."

Great, Kristen thought. She watched as Leah pushed hangers from side to side, stopping every now and then to **contemplate** the possibilities of a particular top or skirt, and tried to remain **optimistic,** even as she realized she'd spent more enjoyable Friday nights watching infomercials for various Ronco products: the one for the food **dehydrator,** in particular, was quite **engaging.**

"Ha! I've got it," Leah finally said, emerging from her cave of clothes with an armful of fashions.

Kristen **appraised** the outfit quickly, and, seeing no animal-print spandex, decided it looked **innocuous** enough. *I'll just agree to everything,* she told herself. *Then Leah will be satisfied.* "Lay it on me," she said, ready to behave like a good little fashionista.

---

scrutinizing: inspecting or examining
countenance: expression or demeanor
squabbling: quarreling
apparel: clothes or garments

opt: choose
endure: suffer patiently
contemplate: ponder or consider
optimistic: positive or cheerful
dehydrator: dryer

engaging: absorbing or fascinating
appraised: evaluated or assessed
innocuous: harmless

"Okay, you didn't want to go 'ho, so we're going to go hippie, instead," Leah said, **beaming**. "First, we have the pants—low-rise boot-cut jeans, kind of like the ones you were wearing, except that these are embroidered and they'll fit a little tighter."

Kristen nodded. "Cool." A little tighter she could handle, and the embroidery *was* kind of neat.

"Next, the shirt," Leah continued. She held out a simple white peasant blouse with short sleeves, a flowing body, and tiny flowers—which complimented the ones on the jeans perfectly—embroidered along the wide neckline. "What do you think?"

"It's great," Kristen said, thankful that her friend hadn't presented her with another skintight tank. In fact, this top was even kind of cute.

Kristen pulled on the pants, which were definitely tighter than the ones she'd had on before—they required a bit of extra effort to zip—and slipped the top over her head. Then she stepped into the shoes and started toward the mirror to check it all out.

"Wait," Leah called. She gathered Kristen's hair and twisted it into an updo, **securing** it with a hair clip. Then she passed Kristen a pair of dangly beaded earrings and, while Kristen put them on, fastened a matching choker around her neck. "Okay—now look," Leah said.

Kristen walked to the mirror and gazed at her reflection, surprised to see that Leah's **alterations** to her clothing and hair had actually enhanced her **appearance**. "Hey," she said, "this actually looks pretty good."

"What did you expect?" Leah asked.

"I don't know," Kristen shrugged. "I guess I just didn't think it would make much of a difference, you know? But I have to admit, I look a lot better now than I did when I got here."

---

beaming: shining
securing: fastening

alterations: changes or modifications

appearance: look or bearing

Leah smiled, obviously pleased with the **transformation**, and Kristen knew that she'd said all the right things. For once.

"So, should we get going?" Kristen asked.

"Definitely," Leah said. "It's almost nine now, so the party should be started. I'm so psyched that you're coming," she added as the two of them started down the stairs. "This is going to make things so much better."

"What do you mean?" Kristen asked.

"Oh, nothing," Leah said. "Just, you know—the stuff we were talking about the other day. The fact that you haven't been around a lot lately and that Tracy's been talking about you a lot."

"Tracy's been—?"

"We're leaving, Mom," Leah called as she opened the front door. Kristen exhaled sharply, swallowing her question until Leah was finished with her mother.

"Okay," Mrs. McDonnell shouted from the kitchen. "Have a good time—and be back by 1 A.M."

"I will," Leah called back. "Stupid curfew," she muttered to Kristen on her way out the door. "What time is yours?"

"Same," Kristen said, although actually, her mother hadn't given her one. "So what were you saying about Tracy? She's been talking about me?"

"Yeah, I thought I told you that the other day," Leah said, heading for her mom's red Subaru.

"Well, you didn't," Kristen said. "You said you thought she was a little bent out of shape because of what Luke said at Stephanie's party, but—"

"Oh," Leah said. "Well, it's really not a big deal anyway," she said with a **dismissive** wave. She climbed into the car and shut her door so that Kristen had to hop into the passenger seat in order to continue the conversation.

---

transformation: metamorphosis

dismissive: disdainful

"It's **significant** to me," Kristen interrupted. "So what did she say?"

Leah turned to face Kristen. "Are you sure you want to know?" Kristen nodded. "Okay, fine. Basically, she just said she's sick of how you act like you're, well, better than all of us. Like with this Trevor thing, and the way you never hang out anymore."

Kristen nodded, pressing her lips together. "Okay," she said softly. "Leah—why didn't you tell me this before?"

"Because I knew you'd make a big deal out of it," Leah said.

"It *is* a big deal. Tracy's saying stuff about me, and now I'm supposed to go to a party at her boyfriend's house and pretend that everything's okay?"

"Everything *is* okay," Leah said. "She only said it because she was feeling **vulnerable** about what Luke said, and no one took her seriously."

"Are you sure?"

"Yes, I'm sure."

Right, Kristen thought. So then why were they all talking about her behind her back in the first place? Everyone was so **duplicitous**. Sometimes she didn't even know why she bothered.

"Are you ready to go?" Leah asked.

Kristen bit her lip. Luke's party was about the last place she wanted to be right now, but she didn't feel like she had much of a choice. Skipping the party would only make things worse. "Yeah, I'm ready," she said.

"Good." Leah turned the key in the ignition and backed out of the driveway. "This is going to be fun, you know," she said, shifting the car into drive. "Really," she added when Kristen didn't respond. "Just forget about what Tracy said—she probably doesn't even remember saying it. And besides, tonight, once she sees you hanging out with the whole crew, it will be like old times. She'll forget all about this thing with Luke—you'll see."

---

significant: important or meaningful   **vulnerable:** sensitive   **duplicitous:** deceitful

"Yeah," Kristen muttered, even though she thought Leah was being overly **sanguine**. When Tracy was upset about something, she didn't let it go easily—especially when it came to Luke. Just last month she'd practically **crucified** a sophomore girl who'd had the nerve to flirt with him at the snack stand during a basketball game. Tracy had **mocked** the poor girl **relentlessly** every time she'd **encountered** her in the hallway, the bathroom, the cafeteria—everywhere.

Still, maybe there was some **veracity** to what Leah was saying. Attending the party and hanging out with everybody would help. She could do a little repair work on her relationship with Tracy and get in the necessary bonding time with Leah, Steph, and everyone else. And then, after making her appearance and performing the friendship **maintenance** she'd been neglecting for a while now, she might even be off the hook for a week or two, which would mean more time for surfing.

*　　*　　*　　*　　*

"You two look *so* cute together," Tracy confided, slinging her arm around Kristen's shoulder.

"Really?" Kristen asked, crinkling up her nose.

"Uh-huh. Totally," Tracy assured her, a wide grin stretching across her face.

With her second beer of the night in her hand, Kristen smiled back. Trevor had never seemed all that attractive to her before, but now, watching him **converse** with Luke on the other side of the room, all the while **sneaking** looks back at her, Kristen had to admit she was feeling somewhat **smitten**. Or at least, she was trying to—trying to just let go for once and do what her friends wanted.

---

sanguine: confident or optimistic
crucified: tormented or humiliated
mocked: teased or ridiculed

relentlessly: persistently or mercilessly
encountered: met or seen
veracity: accuracy or truthfulness

maintenance: upkeep
converse: speak
sneaking: stealing
smitten: fascinated or enthralled

"How's it going?" Leah asked, **rejoining** Kristen and Tracy by the fireplace. As they turned to face her, both Kristen and Tracy lost their balance and leaned into one another, giggling.

"Everything's awesome, Leah," Kristen said, raising her beer.

"Absolutely fabulous," Tracy agreed. She lifted her drink too, and bumped it into Kristen's, spilling beer on the floor and sending them both into another fit of laughter.

"O-kay," Leah said. "It looks like you two are having a pretty good time."

"The best," Tracy **declared**, and then she turned to Kristen. "You know, I was mad at you before, but I'm totally over it now. I love hanging out with you."

"Me too," Kristen said, grinning. "I'm a lot of fun." She stared at Tracy for a minute, and then both of them burst out laughing again.

"Well, just so you know, it's about midnight now, so we're going to have to leave in another half hour, okay?"

Kristen shook her head. "I don't have to be home till two," she said, extending her index and middle finger while **clumsily** holding onto her beer with the same hand.

"I thought you said your curfew was one o'clock," Leah said.

Kristen shrugged. "I lied."

"Excellent—then that gives you plenty of time for a tour of Luke's house, doesn't it?"

Kristen felt someone's arms **encircle** her and was surprised to see that Trevor had somehow managed to **discreetly** cross the room. She glanced at the spot where she'd seen him last. "When did you—?"

"I snuck up on you while you were talking to Leah," he said, wrapping his arms more tightly around her and kissing her on the cheek. Kristen smiled and leaned into him. It felt good to be held. "So what do you say? Do you want a tour?" Trevor asked.

---

rejoining: reuniting   **clumsily:** awkwardly   **discreetly:** unnoticeably
declared: announced   **encircle:** surround

Kristen looked at Leah, whose eyebrows were raised impossibly high, and giggled. "What kind of tour?" she asked.

"The kind of tour where I show you where all the rooms are—the kitchen, the bathroom"—Trevor placed his mouth next to Kristen's ear and added—"the *bedrooms*."

Again Kristen glanced at Leah, who had cocked her head and was now squinting at her. It seemed like a face Kristen's mother might make, and it made Kristen giggle again.

"So, what do you think?" Trevor whispered. The **sensation** of his lips and his breath so close to her ear sent shivers down Kristen's spine.

"Okay," she said, turning around to face Trevor, who didn't let his arms drop from around her body for a second.

"Kristen, we have to leave in like fifteen minutes," Leah said.

"Someone else can give her a ride home," Tracy replied.

"I don't know if that's—"

"Yeah, someone else can give me a ride home," Kristen agreed carelessly. She took a big gulp from her beer, made an effort to steady herself, then looked up at Trevor, whose eyes seemed to be twinkling more and more as the night wore on. "Let's go," she said, taking him by the hand.

Trevor shot a look at Luke, who was still standing on the other side of the room, and chuckled. "All right," he said, and together the two of them headed for the staircase. As they started up, Kristen tripped over the first step, **erupted** into laughter, and waved back at Tracy.

"Have a good time," Tracy called, waving and giggling back at her.

"We will," Kristen shouted. "See you later, Leah," she added, but Trevor scooted her up the stairs before she was able to hear Leah's reply.

---

sensation: awareness or feeling   **erupted:** exploded or burst

"So this is the second floor," Trevor said when they reached the landing.

"Very nice," Kristen replied, smiling.

"Yes, you are," Trevor said, leaning down to kiss her.

Kristen felt his smooth lips press gently into hers and sighed. "Mmmm."

"As for the rest of the tour," he said **hastily**, "that's the bathroom, that's Luke's parents' room, that's his older sister's room." Trevor gestured, **indicating** each one in turn. "And this one right here," he added, pulling her into the room on their right, "is Luke's."

"Wow," Kristen said as she walked in farther. "This is clean."

Trevor laughed. "Yeah, that's a surprise, right?"

"I leave a lot of *flothes* on the cloor—I mean *clothes* on the floor!" Kristen corrected herself, laughing.

"Do you?" Trevor asked, coming closer to her again and putting his arms around her waist.

"Mm-hmm." Kristen nodded. "I've got two different homes, you know. Hard to keep my stuff neat when I'm always going back and forth. . . ." She trailed off, suddenly feeling a wave of sadness. No, she wasn't going to let herself think about that now, any of it. She was here with Trevor—Trevor, who could make her forget about her parents.

"You look really nice tonight," Trevor said, kissing the top of her head. Then he leaned in and began kissing her ear. Kristen shrunk back at first, nervous, but then let her head drop back, allowing Trevor to continue kissing around her neck and down to her collarbone. "I love this shirt on you," he said, sliding his hand underneath the fabric and up her spine.

Kristen gasped, but Trevor kept kissing her. "*Trevor*," Kristen whispered, barely able to catch her breath.

---

hastily: quickly   indicating: pointing

"You feel so amazing," he said, brushing his lips along the low neckline of her shirt. He massaged the small of her back, his fingertips against the top of her jeans.

Her entire body was tingling now. It felt incredible, but it also felt like everything was happening so fast that she couldn't keep up, and before Kristen even knew what was going on, Trevor's hand was at her jeans, trying to push its way inside.

"Trevor," she said, louder this time as she grabbed his wrist.

"What's wrong?" he asked as she pulled his hand free from its **viselike** grip on her jeans.

Kristen shook her head. "I don't know, I just—"

"Doesn't it feel good?"

"Yes, it does," she said. "I'm just not sure I'm ready—"

Trevor **snickered**. "Oh come on. You're not telling me you're a virgin, are you? Because I don't buy that for one second." Trevor pulled her closer and started to kiss her again. At first Kristen let him—his body did feel so warm next to hers—but every time she tried to slow things down a little by pulling back or kissing him more softly, he pressed into her harder and held her more **resolutely**.

"Trevor, I don't want to . . . get too serious," she said. Then she felt his hand undoing the button on her jeans and pulling down the zipper. "Trevor—I can't!" She was **embarrassed** at first, but then she looked into his eyes.

"What do you mean, you *can't*?" he sneered, and all at once, the eyes that had seemed so soft just ten minutes ago appeared cold and mocking.

"I just—I don't feel right about this," Kristen said, backing away from him. But as she **retreated**, he **advanced**.

"Come on, Kristen. Don't be such a prude."

Kristen winced. Trevor's **abrupt** language had **expunged** every last **vestige** of the passion Kristen had been feeling, and suddenly,

---

viselike: unrelenting or powerful
snickered: laughed
resolutely: firmly

embarrassed: uncomfortable
retreated: withdrew
advanced: proceeded

abrupt: curt or brusque
expunged: destroyed
vestige: trace

she felt **exceedingly** sober—mentally, at least. "You know," she said, "I really don't feel right about it. At least not with you."

"Then why'd you come up with me? And why have you been teasing me all night?" Trevor demanded.

"I haven't been teasing you," Kristen said. She backed toward the hallway, but Trevor swung the door shut and pressed her up against it.

"You came up here to be with me," he said. "And everyone saw you do it. So why don't you just loosen up and finish what you started?"

"Trevor, I—" Kristen started, but he pressed his mouth against hers so hard that she couldn't speak. And when she tried to push him away, he grabbed her wrists and pinned them against the door. For a moment, Kristen froze there, **passive**, but as Trevor moved his lips from her mouth to her neck and chest, she brought her knee up into his groin as fast and **forcibly** as she could.

"Ow!" Trevor groaned, doubling over, and as he did, Kristen opened the door and sprinted down the steps. She looked for Tracy or Stephanie in the living room, but to her surprise, the entire crowd seemed to have gone. Just then, she heard voices coming from the back room—loud voices, TV voices. *They must have put on a movie,* Kristen thought, relieved to find that she and Trevor were not in fact alone in the house. She started toward the family room, **anxious** to find one of her friends, but just as she crossed the **threshold** into the dark dining room, she ran smack into someone who'd been coming from the **opposite** direction.

"Kristen?"

"Oh my God, Luke—is Tracy still here?"

"Yeah, she's in the family room watching a movie," Luke said.

"Thanks," Kristen replied, breathing heavily. She was still a bit **winded** from her **skirmish** with Trevor. She started toward the sound of the television, but Luke put his hand on her elbow. "Is

exceedingly: extremely	**anxious:** eager	**winded:** breathless
passive: motionless	**threshold:** entrance	**skirmish:** struggle
forcibly: powerfully	**opposite:** alternate	

something wrong?" he asked. "Hey—you're *shaking*. Are you all right?"

That one simple question asked with **genuine** concern brought a **torrent** of emotion rushing to the surface for Kristen. "I—," she started, but her voice cracked.

"Shhhh," Luke murmured. "It's okay. Come here." He pulled Kristen close, **enveloping** her in his arms. Kristen **started** at first, her body going **rigid**, but as Luke continued to whisper softly, "It's okay, it's okay," she **acquiesced** and let him hold her. His touch was completely different from Trevor's. While Trevor had pawed and grabbed, Luke simply **embraced**. His arms weren't **threatening**, they were **protective**, and his voice wasn't **coercive**, it was comforting. Then, all of a sudden, she was blinded by an explosion of light.

"What's going on in here?" someone demanded. It took Kristen a minute to **recover** her vision, but when she did, she saw Tracy standing next to the light switch with her arms folded across her chest.

"Nothing," Luke said. He let one of his arms drop so he could turn to face Tracy, but he kept his other one solidly around Kristen's shoulders. "Kristen was upset and I was just trying to calm her down."

"By groping her in a dark room?"

Luke let his other arm drop. "I wasn't groping her, Trace—it was a hug. She was shaking," Luke said.

Tracy glared at Kristen. "What was she upset about?" she asked. She spoke as though Kristen wasn't in the room, even though she was staring straight at her.

"I don't know," Luke said, turning to Kristen. "I was just about to ask." Again, he gazed at her with such **authentic** concern that Kristen felt herself drawn to him.

"Well, you don't need to," Tracy said. "She's my friend—I'll take over from here." Luke stood there for a moment, looking back and

---

genuine: sincere
torrent: flood
enveloping: enclosing
started: flinched
rigid: stiff

acquiesced: yielded or agreed
embraced: hugged
threatening: menacing

protective: shielding or guarding
coercive: forceful
recover: regain
authentic: real or genuine

forth between Tracy and Kristen like he wasn't quite sure what to do. "That means you can leave, Luke," Tracy said.

He glanced at Kristen one last time, then left, muttering something about seeing if everyone was still awake or if they'd all passed out by now. Once he was gone, Tracy stepped closer to Kristen. "I don't know what you think you're doing, but you'd better stay the hell away from my boyfriend," she spat.

"Tracy, I—"

"I mean it, Kristen. I know Leah told you what Luke said at Stephanie's party, but you can just forget about it. He was drunk, and he's not interested, so you can stop with the little games."

Kristen was **dumbfounded**. "I'm not playing games, Tracy," she said. "What Luke said was true. I was upset and he was just trying to help."

"Oh, that's right," Tracy said, rolling her eyes. "And just what was it that upset you so much that you needed my boyfriend to **coddle** you? Did Jack Johnson stop recording? Or is the surf low?"

"For your information, your boyfriend's best friend just tried to rape me," Kristen blurted out, tears coming to her eyes.

Tracy's face went blank with shock, then settled back into an **antagonistic** glare. "I *saw* you go up there with him," she said.

"Well, yeah—I went up on my own, but then I wanted to leave and he wouldn't let me. He held me there and—"

"Oh, come on, Kristen. Is this the story you fed Luke to get him to wrap his arms around you?"

Kristen swallowed, unable to believe the way Tracy was reacting. "Actually, I was on my way to find you—*my friend*—because I thought you'd understand and be able to help me."

"Help you *what*? Get away from Trevor?" Tracy **craned** her neck and stared over Kristen's shoulder. "He's not exactly in hot **pursuit**—is he even still here?"

---

dumbfounded: puzzled   **antagonistic:** hostile   **pursuit:** chase
coddle: pamper   **craned:** stretched

Kristen blinked. "I—I don't know." She cast a nervous glance toward the stairs.

Tracy hesitated for a moment, squinting at Kristen with **uncertainty**. Then she folded her arms across her chest again, shifting her weight so that her right hip jutted out **defiantly**. "Did you plan this?" she asked.

"Plan what? To come here and almost get raped?"

"You can drop the rape story—I don't buy it," Tracy said. "I think you made it up to get attention and to make Luke feel sorry for you."

Kristen shook her head. "Tracy, that's **ludicrous**—"

"Don't even try to **deny** it, Kristen. I know you're jealous of me—you have been for a long time, and it only got worse when I started dating Luke. It's so obvious that you have a thing for him. I mean, God, the way you look at him—you're like a little puppy dog. It's **pathetic**. You must have been so psyched when Leah told you about that stupid comment. You probably thought this party was your big chance to—"

"Oh my God!" Kristen yelled, clenching her fists at her sides. "Are you even listening to yourself? You are *so* **paranoid**. This isn't about you, or Luke, or—"

"Of course it isn't," Tracy interrupted. "It's all about *you*, isn't it? Poor little Kristen, her parents got divorced. Poor little Kristen, her uncle moved away. Poor little Kristen, she's having a hard time. Poor little Kristen, nobody understands her. Well, I'm sick of it, and I'm not going to let you **manipulate** me anymore."

"*Me?*" Kristen gaped. "Manipulate *you*? You've got to be kidding."

"Oh, please," Tracy said. "There's always something wrong with you, and you expect everyone else to put up with it. You never hang around with us anymore, but you still expect us to include you in everything, and then when I try to do something nice and set you up with Luke's best friend, you twist the situation so that you can hit on my boyfriend."

---

uncertainty: doubt or skepticism
defiantly: challengingly

ludicrous: silly or preposterous
deny: dispute

pathetic: tragic
paranoid: delusional
manipulate: control

"Oh, forget it," Kristen said, throwing her hands up in the air. "I don't have to stand here and take this from you."

As she turned to leave, she noticed that a bit of a crowd had started to gather in the kitchen. Obviously all the yelling had interrupted their movie. "I'm leaving," she said to Tracy. "So you can have the spotlight all to yourself, just the way you like it," she added. Then she stormed out the front door and slammed it behind her.

Of course, once she was out in the cold air, it **occurred** to her that she didn't have a ride home. Leah had already left, and she certainly wasn't about to see if Trevor could still give her a lift, which meant she had one **option**: walking.

It's okay, Kristen told herself. *It's not that far. Only about . . .* six miles. Halfway down Luke's driveway, the reality of just how far that was—and how **frigid** it was outside—hit her, and for a moment she considered going back into the house to see if there was anyone else who might be headed back toward town. But after such a dramatic exit, she would have felt like a complete **imbecile** walking back in. So, **determined** not to make a fool of herself and **wagering** that sooner or later someone would happen by and offer to pick her up, Kristen set out along the road.

Fifteen minutes into her walk, she began to question her decision. Not a single car had passed in either direction yet, and her feet were already beginning to feel numb. *This is stupid,* she told herself. *Just go back and get somebody to drive you.* Abruptly, she switched direction and started back toward Luke's. But the thought that had **persuaded** her to turn around was quickly followed by a new one.

What are you, an idiot? she wondered, stopping in her tracks. *You can't go back in there—you'll look like the biggest **lunatic** ever!* Again, Kristen changed direction and started back down the road toward her mother's house. She turned around three more times over the next five minutes, **grappling** with the consequences of

---

occurred: struck	**imbecile:** idiot	**persuaded:** convinced
option: choice	**determined:** adamant	**lunatic:** madman
frigid: freezing	**wagering:** betting	**grappling:** wrestling

returning to the party versus continuing onward, and **lamenting** how stupid she was with each **successive** decision, until finally she saw a set of headlights on the horizon.

"Thank God. Just please don't let it be Trevor. Let it be anyone but Trevor," she **supplicated** as the car approached. "Or Tracy," she added. And when the blue and white lights went on, she knew she'd gotten her wish.

The police car pulled up behind her on the dirt shoulder and stopped, its headlights and a bright spotlight **illuminating** the world around her for a good forty feet. "Everything okay, miss?" a voice called to her from somewhere behind the lights.

Kristen shielded her eyes and squinted. "Yup. I'm just . . . getting some fresh air." She heard footsteps on the gravel and could just make out the **silhouette** of a large man, about 6' 3" and at least two hundred pounds, approaching.

"Where are you headed tonight?" the silhouette asked when he was about six feet away. Backlit by all the lights on the police car, he looked almost **extraterrestrial** standing there, especially since Kristen was still a bit buzzed.

"I'm just going home," Kristen said.

"And where would that be?" the alien asked her.

"To my mom's—in town." The silence that followed this statement made Kristen feel as though more information was **requisite**. "Sixty-four Coach Lantern Lane," she added, hoping to **demonstrate** how **cooperative** she could be.

"That's a long way from here," he replied, "nearly ten miles. Are you aware that it's only twenty-two degrees outside and that a ten-mile walk would take you **approximately** three and a half hours?"

Kristen swallowed hard. "I . . . like to walk," she said finally. "And I don't get cold easily."

"Have you been drinking at all tonight, miss?"

---

lamenting: regretting
successive: continuous
supplicated: begged
illuminating: lighting

silhouette: outline
extraterrestrial: alien
requisite: necessary
demonstrate: show

cooperative: collaborative or helpful
approximately: almost

Kristen brought her hand to her face. It didn't seem **judicious** to answer this particular question. "Um . . . I don't think so," she said.

"You don't think so?"

"Well, I had a few mixed drinks, you know, with a lot of different kinds of fruit juice and stuff?" she lied. "And I guess there may have been alcohol in some of those, but I'm not really sure."

"Your breath actually smells like beer," the officer told her. "Do you remember having any beer tonight?"

Again, Kristen decided **ignorance** was her best **strategy**. "I don't think so."

He didn't seem satisfied with her answer. "Tell you what—why don't you hop in the car and I'll give you a ride."

"That's okay," she said. "I don't mind walking—really."

"Actually, miss, I'm going to ask you to get in the car. As I'm sure you know, underage drinking is **unlawful** in this state, and while I don't **intend** to charge you with anything tonight, I do want to make sure you get home safely."

"Oh," Kristen said. She felt the police officer's hand on her elbow and allowed him to steer her toward his cruiser. As he was settling her in backseat, she got an idea. "Hey, if you aren't planning to charge me or anything," she said, "do you think maybe you could drop me off down the street from my mom's and let me walk home from there?"

The officer, whose nameplate said Officer Doyle, smiled at her. "I said I wasn't going to charge you," he said, "but I didn't say I was letting you off the hook." Then he closed the door, leaving Kristen in the dark, staring at the metal grate that separated the front seat from the back, with just one thought in her head: *My mother is going to **annihilate** me.*

---

judicious: wise   strategy: plan   intend: mean or plan
ignorance: inexperience unlawful: illegal   annihilate: kill

Chapter Five

The closer in **proximity** Officer Doyle got to Kristen's mother's apartment, the louder the pounding in Kristen's head became. *She's going to have a fit,* Kristen kept thinking. At least she wasn't being **indicted**, so there wouldn't be any sort of **monetary penalty** to **quarrel** about. And if she could **finesse** it just right, she might be able to keep her mom from going completely ballistic.

"I just need to make a quick stop at the station," Officer Doyle told her, pulling his cruiser into the **subterranean** parking garage beneath police headquarters. "You can wait here," he said, hopping out of the car. As he walked away, he pointed his key chain back toward the car and pressed a button, **eliciting** a familiar *beep-beep* sound. Kristen **deduced** that he must have activated some kind of alarm system that would sound if anyone tried to get in—*or out*—of the car, so she just **reclined** against the black leather seat and waited.

After a minute, she let her head drop back and closed her eyes, but she had to open them again immediately when the image of Trevor **confining** her in the doorway of Luke's bedroom appeared in her mind.

"What were you thinking, anyway?" a shrill voice demanded, causing Kristen to jump. At first she thought the question was directed at her—she'd just been **speculating** the same thing herself. But when she turned to look out the back window of the cruiser, she saw a fortyish woman in a bright orange parka walking alongside a teenage boy dressed all in black.

"**Defacing** public property—your school, no less," the woman continued in a disgusted tone. "What would make you pull a stunt

proximity: nearness	**finesse:** maneuver	**confining:** restraining or
indicted: charged	**subterranean:** underground	restricting
monetary: fiscal	**eliciting:** evoking	**speculating:** thinking
penalty: price	**deduced:** concluded	**defacing:** damaging
quarrel: argue	**reclined:** leaned	

like that, anyway? Haven't you gotten yourself into enough trouble? Haven't you embarrassed your father and me enough?"

Kristen squinted at the boy, who said nothing but kept his gaze focused straight ahead and his expression blank. He seemed familiar, but the light was **subdued** and she couldn't quite place him.

"Well, don't just stare like that, Nate—answer me," the woman commanded him, and that's when Kristen figured it out. It was Nate Jacobs, a junior at Adams. Kristen rarely encountered him. She was on the college prep track, and he took mostly vocational courses. They'd been going to school together since eighth grade, when he'd moved to New Hampshire from New York, but he'd always been somewhat of an outsider, and Kristen had never bothered to try to meet anyone outside of her particular social circle.

"I want an answer," repeated the woman, who had to be Nate's mother. She stopped ten feet away from the police car Kristen was in and stared at her son. "What were you doing spray-painting Elvis Presley's head on the side of the school?"

Kristen clapped her hand to her mouth to keep herself from laughing and ducked as low as she could without **obscuring** her view.

"Well? I'm waiting," Mrs. Jacobs said, crossing her arms.

Slowly, Nate turned to face her, his expression still blank and completely **unapologetic**. Kristen was struck by how dark his features were—his hair, his eyebrows, his eyes—and of course they were all **accentuated** by the shadows cast by the yellow parking garage lights. He gazed at his mother for another moment, then shrugged. "It was **bland**," he said.

"It was bland?" his mother cried. "That's all you have to say? It was *bland*?" Nate continued to stare. "And what? You thought a nice portrait of Elvis would **spruce** it up?"

"He *is* the King," Nate said, the corner of his mouth curving upward ever so slightly.

---

subdued: moderate
obscuring: hiding or
blocking

unapologetic: unremorseful
accentuated: emphasized

bland: boring
spruce: tidy

"What am I going to do with you, Nate?" Mrs. Jacobs lamented, **kneading** her forehead with one hand.

That was it. Kristen couldn't **suppress** her amusement any longer. She started to laugh out loud—at **precisely** the same moment that the car lights came on and the *beep-beep* of the cruiser's alarm system caused both Nate and his mother to turn and stare directly at her.

"Oh my God," Kristen whispered, sinking down in the backseat. Just then Officer Doyle opened the door and leaned in.

"Did I miss anything?" he asked.

Kristen peeked out from between her hands. "Are they gone?"

"Yes."

Slowly Kristen eased herself up and glanced out the back window. The space where Nate and his mother had been standing was bathed in yellow light and shadows. "Do you think they saw me?"

"Oh, yeah, they saw you," Officer Doyle **confirmed** as he slid into the front seat and started the car.

"This night just keeps getting better," she said, slumping back in her seat.

"Ready to finish it off?" Officer Doyle asked, backing out. Kristen didn't bother to answer. She figured it was a **rhetorical** question anyway—it wasn't like she had a choice in the matter.

Damn, she thought. *Why did Nate have to see me?* She would have preferred to have kept her **pseudo** arrest quiet. But then again, who did she think Nate would tell? He didn't exactly hang with anyone from Kristen's crowd. He didn't exactly hang with *anyone.* Who would listen to him? *No one,* Kristen realized, and she felt a little better. At least she hadn't been spotted by someone **crucial**.

It only took five minutes to reach Kristen's mother's apartment. She'd never realized just how close they lived to the police station. Officer Doyle pulled into the small lot next to the apartment building and opened Kristen's door for her.

---

kneading: rubbing
suppress: control
precisely: exactly

confirmed: verified
rhetorical: artificial or contrived

pseudo: false
crucial: important or significant

"Ready?" he asked.

"Guess so," Kristen replied.

When they reached the front door, Kristen started to get out her key and open it, but Officer Doyle stopped her. "I prefer to knock," he said. "It wouldn't be right for me to come in without your mother's **permission**."

"Oh," Kristen said. "Okay." She stepped back and let him do his thing.

It took three rounds of knocking to bring her mother to the door, and when she opened it she still looked half asleep. However, when she took in Officer Doyle's large frame in the doorway, her eyes sprang open.

"What's wrong? What's happened?" she blurted. "Where's my daughter? Is she okay?"

"Everyone is fine, Mrs. Carmichael," Officer Doyle said, assuming—**erroneously**—that Kristen and her mother would share the same last name.

"It's Graham," Kristen's mother said, gathering her flannel robe more tightly around her neck. "Hannah Graham."

"Hannah Graham?" Officer Doyle said. "From channel eight?"

"That's right," Kristen's mother said, smiling her coy "yes it's me-and-I'm-famous" smile and batting her eyelashes. But her **digression** into local-**celebrity** mode only lasted a second. As soon as she glanced back up at Officer Doyle, standing in full uniform and nearly filling her doorway, her mouth fell back into a concerned straight line, the corners slightly turned down. "Excuse me, Officer . . . Doyle," she said, smiling as she located his nameplate. "May I ask why you're here?"

"Oh, yes Ms. Graham, of course. I'm sorry."

Kristen rolled her eyes. Sure, her mother was attractive, but she didn't understand why men **consistently** fell all over themselves in her presence. It wasn't like she was a supermodel in a bikini.

---

permission: approval
erroneously: mistakenly

digression: drifting or detour
celebrity: star

consistently: frequently or often

"I'm here because your daughter, Kristen," he said, stepping aside so that Kristen's mother could see her, "had a little too much to drink tonight and was attempting to walk home from Briar Street."

"Briar Street?" Ms. Graham repeated. "It's below freezing outside. Kristen—what were you thinking?"

I wasn't thinking, I was drinking, popped into Kristen's mind, but instead she just shrugged.

"Now, I'm not charging your daughter with anything tonight, even though it is **illegal** for minors to drink, of course."

"Of course," Kristen's mother said, as though the mere mention of underage drinking offended her delicate **sensibilities**. Kristen wondered what Officer Doyle would think if he knew that Kristen had caught her mother—the upstanding Hannah Graham—making out with her coanchor boyfriend on their living room sofa.

"But I did want to get her home safely and make you aware that she was engaging in risky behavior," Officer Doyle continued.

Kristen's mom reached out and touched his forearm while gazing directly into his eyes. "Thank you," she said. Officer Doyle blushed.

"Just doing my job, Ms. Graham," he said.

"Call me Hannah."

"Okay. *Hannah*," Officer Doyle replied.

Kristen felt a swirl of nausea. "She has a boyfriend," Kristen said, pushing her way past Officer Doyle and into the apartment.

"Kristen," her mother barked. "Come back here and thank Officer Doyle for getting you home safely."

"It's, uh, Ted," Officer Doyle said.

"Thanks, Ted," Kristen called.

"Kristen!" her mother said.

"Sorry. Thanks . . . *Officer Doyle*," Kristen corrected herself. Then she headed for her bedroom. Her mother could certainly handle

---

illegal: unlawful

sensibilities: emotions or tastes

the police on her own—she seemed to be quite the expert, Kristen thought to herself **acrimoniously**.

Within seconds, her mother was standing in her doorway. "Kristen Graham Carmichael—what do you have to say for yourself?" she demanded.

"I didn't get arrested and I got home safely?" Kristen offered.

"No thanks to yourself," her mother replied. "On either count. What were you thinking, anyway? And where were you drinking tonight? I thought you went out with Leah, to a movie or something. Isn't that what you told me?"

"Mom—"

"Forget it, Kristen. I don't want to hear any excuses right now. Do you know how **humiliating** this is for me? That police officer recognized me, and now he's going to go back to his station and tell everyone that he had to bring Hannah Graham's daughter home because she was **inebriated**. This could be very bad publicity for me."

"You're the one who told him your name," Kristen reminded her. "He thought you were Mrs. Carmichael."

"He would have recognized me **eventually** anyway—but that's not the point."

What is *the point?* Kristen wondered. She contemplated telling her mother about Trevor but decided against it. She wouldn't want to embarrass her mother further by being an attempted rape victim, besides being a drunk. Surely it would be too much for Hannah Graham, KJKF News, to handle.

"The point is that you've behaved very irresponsibly tonight. Not only did you **compromise** my position as a **reputable** news anchor but also you put yourself into a **precarious** situation."

Oh, you mean I factor in there somewhere? Kristen thought.

"But it's too late for us to talk about this now. I'm **exhausted**, you're exhausted, and we should both get some sleep before we

---

acrimoniously: bitterly
humiliating: disgraceful or shaming

inebriated: intoxicated or drunk
eventually: ultimately
compromise: endanger

reputable: respected
precarious: risky
exhausted: tired

discuss the poor choices you made tonight. You can, however, consider yourself very grounded for the next two weeks, young lady, and I'll be passing that information on to your father as well."

Kristen's mother shot her a hard look, which Kristen returned and held until her mother looked away.

"So . . . we'll talk about this in the morning," her mom said. "Get some sleep," she added, and then she turned and walked down the hall to her own room, where Kristen heard **distinctly** male mumblings **interspersed** with her mother's muffled voice.

As soon as she was gone, Kristen finally let herself do what she'd needed to do all night—she sank onto her bed and just cried.

distinctly: uniquely   **interspersed:** scattered

When Kristen walked into school on Monday morning, something felt different—something beyond the remains of the throbbing headache she was *still* nursing from all that drinking on Friday night.

At first she wasn't sure what it was, but after a couple of classes it became obvious. Everywhere she went, conversations **ceased** and whispers **commenced**. At first she thought she was being paranoid, but when she started down the junior wing for French class and someone made a police siren noise, which was followed by **plentiful** giggling and pointing in her general direction, she realized it wasn't her imagination.

"Leah," she whispered, sliding into the vacant seat next to her friend, "what's going on?"

Leah gazed over at Kristen with the expression of a small child who'd been caught stealing a cookie but wasn't quite ready to **confess** her **transgression**. "What do you mean?" she asked, her voice **wavering**. Leah had always been a **dreadful** liar.

"Just tell me," Kristen said. "I know you know. Everyone's looking at me funny everywhere I go. Is there some kind of rumor going around or something?" *Did Nate Jacobs actually tell people he saw me?* she wondered. Had people actually listened to him?

Leah screwed up her face into an expression that was one part pity and one part **recrimination**, but before she had a chance to speak, Madame de Gaulle entered the room and started class. Kristen tapped her feet and chewed her pencil for what felt like an **eternity** as Ms. De Gaulle lectured **relentlessly** on dictation,

ceased: stopped	**transgression:** offense	**recrimination:** mutual
commenced: began	**wavering:** faltering	accusation
plentiful: ample	**dreadful:** horrible	**eternity:** endlessness
confess: disclose		**relentlessly:** unstoppably

vocabulary review, irregular verb conjugations, and even a French spelling bee, but finally the bell rang and it was time for lunch.

"Okay, lay it on me," Kristen said, bolting out of the room behind Leah. "What's going on?"

Leah stopped next to the nearest bank of lockers and stepped out of the major hallway traffic lanes. Then she sighed heavily and shook her head at Kristen. "Everyone knows," she said, as if those two words explained everything.

"About the police?" Kristen whispered.

"Yeah, and also . . . everything else," Leah replied.

Kristen scrunched her eyebrows together. "What do you mean, 'everything else'?" she asked. Had everyone heard about Trevor trying to rape her too? And about Tracy getting **fanatical** about Luke? Then why hadn't Leah called to see if she were okay?

Leah rolled her eyes and seemed **exasperated**. "I mean everything *else*," she said. Kristen gave Leah a blank stare—she still wasn't completely sure just how much had gotten around, but Leah didn't seem to care. "Come on, Kristen. You can't expect to have as wild a night as that and not have people talk about it," she said. "I still can't believe, you and Trevor. *And* the other guy. I thought you said you weren't ready yet."

Kristen took a step back. "What did you say?" she asked, **staggered** by what she thought she'd just heard.

"You heard me," Leah **admonished** her. "And there's no point in denying it. Everybody knows what happened, Kristen."

"Yeah, everyone except *me*," Kristen said. "Leah—what are you talking about?"

Leah ran one hand through her short, **auburn** hair and glanced at the ceiling. "Why are you making me do this?"

"Do what?" Kristen asked.

"Tell you what you already know," Leah said. "Are you some kind of **sadist** or something? Do you like making me uncomfortable?"

---

fanatical: rabid	**staggered:** surprised	**auburn:** reddish brown
exasperated: irritated	**admonished:** warned	**sadist:** beast or savage

"Leah, I swear—I have no idea what you're talking about. Please, just tell me what people are saying," Kristen pleaded.

Leah stared into her friend's brown eyes for a moment, her own green eyes tired and disappointed, then slumped back against the lockers. "Fine. I'll say it," Leah said. "I heard that you slept with Trevor, and then, when he told you that it was just a casual thing and he didn't want to be your boyfriend or anything, you got all upset and stormed out of the room."

"Is that what he said?" Kristen asked. But Leah didn't answer. She just stared straight ahead **vapidly**, like she was reciting items off a shopping list she'd memorized.

"Then you went downstairs and cornered Luke while everyone else was watching a movie and tried to convince him that—" Leah stopped and stared down at her shoes.

"What?" Kristen demanded. "Tell me what you heard."

"You cornered Luke and told him that . . . that you wanted him and that you could do things that Tracy had never even heard of."

"Oh my God!" Kristen said. "Are you serious?"

"Then, when Tracy came in and found you trying to kiss Luke, you started yelling at her about how she didn't deserve him and how much better off he'd be with you, and then . . ." Leah let her voice trail off, but Kristen had to hear it all.

"What?" Kristen asked.

"*Well . . . ,*" Leah started, but she clearly didn't want to finish. She looked to her left and then to her right, **presumably** for an excuse to escape the rest of the conversation, but Kristen wasn't about to let her go. She grabbed Leah's upper arm and **urged** her onward.

"Tell me. What is it? What else are people saying?"

"Just that . . . well . . . that after you left the party, you took a taxi to this club called the Station and hooked up with some guy from

---

vapidly: dully or insipidly   **presumably:** probably   **urged:** encouraged

Derry High, and then the two of you got picked up by the police for
. . . well . . . for, you know, in a public place and everything."

"I—he—we—*what*?" Kristen said.

"Look, Kristen, I know this can't all be true," Leah said. Her gaze
flicked around the hallway, then she lowered her voice. "But some
of it . . . I mean, I saw you heading upstairs with Trevor. It didn't
exactly look like you were going to play Monopoly."

"Yeah, but—"

"And a lot of people heard you fighting with Tracy over Luke."

"We weren't fighting *over* Luke," Kristen said. "At least, *I* wasn't.
Tracy was acting all paranoid and claiming that—"

"Trevor knows the guy from Derry," Leah said quietly.

"What guy from Derry?" Kristen demanded.

"The guy you met at the Station. He and Trevor are good
friends—that's how Trevor heard about it." Kristen shook her head.
She couldn't believe what she was hearing. "His name is Matt Gray
and he's a receiver for Derry," Leah continued. "Trevor met him at a
football clinic over the summer."

"Leah!" Kristen shouted. "I can't believe you. Just because
Trevor knows some guy from Derry, that doesn't mean I hooked up
with him. Trevor tried to rape me, for God's sake—are you really
going to take his word over mine?"

Again, Leah glanced past Kristen at the students passing by in
the hallway, biting her lip. They all seemed to be looking at Kristen
with a mix of amusement and **disdain**, but Kristen didn't care. She
was getting used to it. Leah, on the other hand, seemed pretty **agitated**.

"Look, Kristen, maybe we should talk about this later," she said,
her eyes darting to every new face that passed by.

"No way," Kristen said, "I want to get this straightened out right
now. First of all, I didn't sleep with Trevor. I kissed him, but I didn't
want things to go any further, and I told him so, but he wouldn't let

---

disdain: scorn   **agitated:** disturbed

me leave. So I kneed him in the groin and ran downstairs. Luke was the first person I saw, and he could tell I was upset, so he gave me a hug. Then Tracy walked in and started making all kinds of stupid **accusations**, so I left. I was going to walk home but a police officer stopped, figured out I'd been drinking, and **insisted** on driving me there and talking to my mother, which he did. I got home around two, my mother grounded me, and that's the end of the story. No taxi, no Station, no freak from Derry, nothing."

Once Kristen had finished, she folded her arms and waited for Leah to speak. She needed Leah to know the truth—she needed an **ally** to help her **nip** these rumors in the bud. More important, she needed a *friend* to back her up in all of this. Someone to hug her and tell her it would all be okay, that she wouldn't have any night-mares about Trevor forcing himself on her. But to her surprise, Leah just shrugged.

"What?" Kristen demanded.

"I don't know," Leah said. "It sounds **improbable**. Honestly Kris, I don't know what to believe. I feel like I just don't know you any-more."

Kristen's jaw dropped. "I'm telling you that Trevor tried to *rape* me, and you can't believe that?"

Leah cringed. "Maybe you just got it wrong," she said. "You were pretty drunk, you know. And Trevor's so sweet—he'd never do any-thing like that. I mean, come on, it's not like he has to rape someone if he wants sex, you know?"

Kristen's stomach turned. "You're the one I don't know any-more," she said quietly. "I don't know how I could be friends with someone who could say something so **despicable**."

Leah avoided her gaze, then, without saying another word, just shook her head and walked away.

"Busy weekend, huh, Kristen?"

---

accusations: allegations or charges
insisted: demanded

ally: helpful person
nip: squelch

improbable: unlikely
despicable: contemptible

Kristen whirled around to see Tracy standing behind her. "What do you want?" Kristen said.

Tracy leaned closer, staring Kristen straight in the eye. "See what happens when you mess with other people's boyfriends?" she said, speaking in a voice so low that only Kristen could hear.

"You bitch," Kristen hissed.

Tracy smiled **smugly**. "Better a bitch than a slut like you," she said sweetly. Then she headed down the hall to where Luke was standing with Trevor and a few of his other buddies.

Kristen watched as Tracy looped her arm through Luke's and said something that made the rest of the guys laugh. Trevor shot a look toward Kristen and grinned. After that, the whole group drifted down the hall and around the corner, leaving Kristen on her own. Completely.

*　　*　　*　　*　　*

"Ms. Carmichael—why don't you give it a try? And try to limit your answer to something that doesn't involve urinating canines this time, please," Ms. Fairfield said, receiving a laugh from the class for her oh-so-**clever** remark. She stood there smiling her tight, straight smile and waiting for Kristen to **blunder**, but this time, Kristen knew the answer. She had, after all, been **sequestered** in her room all weekend.

"Macduff," she said. "He's the one who wasn't 'of woman born,' like Macbeth keeps saying."

"And how is that possible?" Ms. Fairfield inquired.

"Because he was . . ." Kristen scanned the lines of act five, scene seven, until she found the quote she was looking for. "Here it is—he was 'from his mother's womb untimely ripped.' His mom had a C-section or something, so he wasn't actually born the way most babies were."

---

smugly: complacently
clever: creative
blunder: flounder
sequestered: isolated

Kristen glanced up at her teacher, contented to see Ms. Fairfield blinking, speechless. "Well, Kristen," she said finally, "it appears that you actually completed the reading for once. I suppose I should **anticipate** seeing pigs fly on my way home tonight as well."

Again the class laughed at Ms. Fairfield's comment, but Kristen wasn't amused. She was having a hard enough time ignoring Trevor, who was sitting beside her, **periodically** telling his friends that she looked completely different with her clothes on, or that she must stuff her bra, because her breasts looked a lot bigger today. She certainly didn't need mockery from her teacher too.

"Wench," Kristen muttered under her breath as her teacher walked to the blackboard.

Ms. Fairfield paused, chalk in midair. "Did you say something, Kristen?" she asked, turning around. She stared directly at Kristen, and Kristen glared back. The classroom was as silent as a morgue. Even Trevor had shut up for once.

"Yes," Kristen said, her gaze unwavering. "I did."

Ms. Fairfield set the chalk in its tray and stepped closer to the student desks. "Would you like to share it with the class?" Ms. Fairfield asked, pursing her lips. Kristen felt the anger rising in her chest and realized that in that moment, she **loathed** the woman standing before her with a passion.

"As a matter of fact, I would," Kristen said, still holding her teacher's gaze. "I called you a wench," she said, being sure to **enunciate** properly.

Ms. Fairfield's thin, smug smile disappeared, and she stared, shocked, for just a moment—her eyes wide, her jaw **slack**—but only for a moment. Then she quickly regained her **poise**, returning her eyes, her mouth, and her jaw to their former **taut** positions. "To the office," she barked, pointing toward the door with one of her long, bony fingers.

---

anticipate: expect
periodically: occasionally or frequently

loathed: hated
enunciate: articulate
slack: loose

poise: composure
taut: rigid

Kristen took her time gathering up her belongings and **strolled** out of the room at her own **pace**. She'd never been kicked out of a class before, but then again, she'd never been the subject of nasty rumors spreading around the school like wildfire, either. It seemed like today was her day for new experiences.

*   *   *   *   *

"Now, Kristen," Mrs. Miller, the principal began, once Ms. Fairfield had taken a seat in one of the **unoccupied** chairs in her office. "Do you understand why Ms. Fairfield sent you down to see me?"

Kristen saw no need for **pretense**. "Mm-hmm. Because I called her a wench, right?"

Mrs. Miller shot a surprised look at Ms. Fairfield, who raised one palm as if to say, *You see what I have to deal with?* "And, uh, Kristen?" Mrs. Miller went on, clearing her throat. "Do you understand why that was wrong?"

"Yes," Kristen said, **wryly**. "It was wrong for the same reason it was wrong of Ms. Fairfield to make fun of *me* in front of the rest of the class."

The principal aimed another concerned glance at Ms. Fairfield before turning back to Kristen with a serious expression. "Now, Kristen, I don't think we need to be **hostile** about this."

"I'm not being hostile," Kristen said. "I'm just telling you the truth. Ms. Fairfield dissed me, so I dissed her."

"Yes. Well." Mrs. Miller took a deep breath and let it out slowly. *Ugh*—just like Kristen's dad always did. Maybe they'd read the same anger management book. "In any case, your behavior **warrants** a three-day suspension, and I—"

"A three-day suspension?" Kristen said. "What about her?" she asked, pointing to her teacher. "What does she get for mocking me? Anything?"

---

strolled: meandered
pace: tempo
unoccupied: empty

pretense: make-believe
wryly: sardonically or ironically

hostile: antagonistic or unfriendly
warrants: justifies

"Please calm down, Kristen," Mrs. Miller said. "We can't have a **meaningful** discussion if you keep yelling and interrupting." Kristen exhaled sharply and slouched back in her chair, crossing her arms. The odds of anything meaningful happening in the company of these two women were **slight** as it was, regardless of whether Kristen yelled, interrupted or stood on her head.

"Thank you," Mrs. Miller said, maintaining **prolonged** eye contact with Kristen while flashing her practiced **administrator** smile. "As I was saying," she went on in what sounded like a talk-radio therapist's voice, "**aggression** toward a teacher warrants a minimum **penalty** of a three-day suspension, which you will be required to serve. Yours will begin as soon as we're able to contact one of your parents to come pick you up."

Kristen snorted. It was one o'clock, and both of her parents were at work and practically impossible to get in touch with. She glanced out the open door at Mrs. Friedman, the secretary, who at that very moment was sitting with the phone to her ear, waiting . . . and waiting . . . and waiting.

She'll be at that all afternoon, Kristen thought, and for a **fleeting** moment, she didn't feel like the absolute unluckiest person in the world. She felt like the second.

* * * * *

A half hour later, Mrs. Friedman still hadn't managed the **herculean** task of getting in touch with either of Kristen's parents. "They must be very busy today," Mrs. Miller said, raising her eyebrows.

They're very busy every *day,* Kristen thought, but she didn't offer this information to her jailer. It was clear from the way Mrs. Miller kept rearranging the papers on her desk that she was beginning to **regret** her decision to have Kristen wait in her office. Several times

---

meaningful: significant or important	**administrator:** manager	**herculean:** superhuman
slight: small	**aggression:** assault	**regret:** rue or lament
prolonged: extended	**penalty:** price	**engage:** involve or interest
	fleeting: passing	

she'd attempted to **engage** Kristen in conversation—"What do you like to do when you're not at school?" and "How long have your parents been divorced?" Stuff like that. She probably believed that with a few well-timed questions she'd have Kristen opening up, spilling her guts, and **repenting** for her **transgressions**. She'd probably seen too many made-for-TV movies.

Kristen had employed "I don't know" as an answer wherever possible and kept her other answers cryptic and **nebulous**, declining to **elaborate** on them, and eventually Mrs. Miller had **relented**. So it was that she'd been stuck reorganizing her already **immaculate** desktop for the last twenty minutes, attempting to look busy and unflustered by the **sullen** teen sitting across from her.

"Well," she said finally, rising from her chair. "I think I'll go see how Mrs. Friedman is doing." Kristen said nothing but instead examined her fingernails. At the **periphery** of her vision, she saw Mrs. Friedman, her ear still glued to the phone, shake her head, at which point Mrs. Miller placed both hands on her hips and said something that included the phrases "where in the world—?" and "how do they expect—?". Kristen was too far away to **discern** anything else.

When Mrs. Miller returned to the office, it appeared as though her smile was losing its battle to stay on her face. "It seems that Mrs. Friedman has encountered a few **obstacles** in trying to contact your parents," she said, her smile **faltering**. "And while I would love to let you stay here, I have another student to see, so I'm going to have to move you to another quiet space. Let's try the guidance office," she said, walking to the door and waiting for Kristen to follow.

The quiet spot Mrs. Miller had chosen was a room within the guidance office that Kristen had never seen before. It was toward the back of the office and off to the side, and they had to walk down a small hallway in order to reach it. "This is Dr. Griffin's room," she

---

repenting: regretting
transgressions: offenses
nebulous: vague
elaborate: expand
relented: yielded

immaculate: spotless
sullen: brooding
periphery: outermost edge of sight
discern: distinguish

obstacles: impediments or barriers
faltering: wavering

said, opening the door. "It's a bit . . . **unorthodox**," she added. And when Kristen walked in, she understood why.

The room, which couldn't have been much more than ten by ten, had wall-to-wall green shag carpet, dark wood-paneled walls, and a light blue ceiling with clouds sponge-painted all over it. For **furnishings**, there were two large, wood-framed chairs with **enormous** square cushions and a matching sofa, all upholstered in the same faded neon orange fabric. On either side of the couch were squat, roughly constructed wooden end tables stained a dark cherry color, and a matching coffee table stretched the length in front of it. Brightly colored beanbag chairs were scattered in the remaining floor space around the **perimeter** of the room, except for one corner, where a padlocked floor-to-ceiling cabinet—also in a dark cherry stain—stood.

Kristen glanced at the bright yellow paper lantern that covered the light fixture hanging from the center of the ceiling, and at the lava lamp—bright pink, with lime green liquid—on the far end table. What *was* this place? And who was this Dr. Griffin the principal had referred to? Kristen didn't remember anyone by that name in the faculty section of any of her yearbooks.

"Why don't you have a seat," Mrs. Miller suggested. "I'll let you know as soon as we reach your parents. You can do some homework while you're waiting." Kristen crossed to the sofa and sat down. As Mrs. Miller exited, she pulled the door half-closed behind her, revealing a five-foot-high poster of a skeleton with a rose in its mouth and the words *American Beauty* written above it in a flowery font. Wow—shag carpet, beanbag chairs, a lava lamp, and a Grateful Dead poster. *This room is **outrageous**,* Kristen thought.

The office appeared to have been decorated in the early seventies and then left untouched—**preserved**, like the childhood rooms of **progeny** who had long since moved away from home.

---

unorthodox: unusual
furnishings: furniture
enormous: huge

perimeter: border(s)
outrageous: preposterous
preserved: maintained

progeny: children

Kristen **chortled**, imagining Mrs. Miller ducking in between meetings for a quick toke. It was even more amusing trying to picture Ms. Fairfield passed out on the tacky orange sofa after a faculty holiday party, photocopies of her butt strewn about the floor. Kristen brought her hand to her mouth to shield the half cough, half laugh this image inspired.

"Hello?"

Kristen jumped at the sight of the large, round, spectacled, balding head peeking around the door. "Sorry—I didn't mean to startle you," the man said. His voice had a slight rasp, and his manner of speaking made him sound both clever and **affable**. "Are you here to see me?" he asked, stepping into the room.

"I don't think so," Kristen said, eyeing him **suspiciously**. He was wearing a rainbow-colored tie-dyed Ben & Jerry's shirt and baggy jeans with Birkenstocks. And though his hairline was indeed **receding**, his salt-and-pepper hair was pulled back into a long, low ponytail that trailed halfway down his back. "Who *are* you?"

"I'm Tom. Tom Griffin," he said, extending a hand. "School psychologist."

Kristen reached up with her right hand and shook **tentatively**. "We have a school psychologist?" she asked.

Dr. Griffin laughed. "More or less," he said. "I work for the whole district, so I split my time between schools. I'm only here about ten hours a week."

"Oh," Kristen said. She gazed down at the green carpet beneath her feet, then back to Dr. Griffin, pausing **momentarily** to gaze at the cyclone of color that was his T-shirt. "Is this, like, your office?" she asked.

"Sort of. I have a desk, a chair, and a file cabinet in the storage closet around the corner, but most of the time I'm in here, meeting with kids, reading, catching up on paperwork. You like it?"

Kristen raised her eyebrows. "It's . . . **unique**," she said.

---

chortled: chuckled
affable: friendly
suspiciously: mistrustfully

receding: dwindling or retreating
tentatively: hesitantly

momentarily: briefly
unique: unusual or remarkable

"You know, I think that's the word people use most to describe this space. I think that's a good thing, don't you?"

"I guess," Kristen said.

Dr. Griffin pulled a key from his pocket and walked over to the tall cabinet. "So . . . what brings you to my interesting room today?" he asked, fidgeting with the padlock.

"I'm just waiting."

Dr. Griffin stopped what he was doing and turned to face her. "For what? Godot?"

Kristen raised one eyebrow. "My parents," she said.

"Ahh." Dr. Griffin nodded slowly, then turned back to the cabinet. After another moment of fidgeting, he managed to pop the lock and swing the doors open, revealing a large boom box, a fairly **extensive** CD collection, a TV-VCR combo, a few videos, some purple yoga mats, red playground balls of **varying** sizes, two shelves of books, assorted art supplies, a couple of stacks of paper, and several bins of Legos, one of which Dr. Griffin **procured** before swinging the doors shut once again.

"So how long is your suspension?" he asked, **affixing** the padlock.

Kristen squinted at him. "I didn't say I was suspended."

"No. But you're here in the guidance office in the middle of the day waiting for your parents," Dr. Griffin said. "If you were sick, you'd be in the nurse's office; if something bad had happened to a family member, you wouldn't be alone; and if you were being **inducted** into the National Honor Society, there would be candles and speeches."

He really thought he was something special, she thought. "Maybe I have a dentist's appointment," she suggested.

Dr. Griffin made the sound of a buzzer on a game show. "*Ernnn!* Those things are scheduled in advance. You wouldn't have to wait

---

extensive: big or wide-ranging

varying: different

procured: got

affixing: fastening

inducted: enrolled

for someone to pick you up—not long enough that they'd send you back here. So how long?"

Okay, so he was pretty quick. "Three days," she conceded.

"Three days," Dr. Griffin repeated. Then he gave Kristen a long stare, as though **assessing** her **qualifications** for a particular job. "That means you either (a) skipped out on a couple of detentions, (b) wrote on the bathroom wall or (c) got into a minor **skirmish** in the hallway."

"*Ernnn!*" Kristen buzzed.

Dr. Griffin raised his eyebrows. "Called a teacher a name?" he guessed. Kristen frowned. Again, Dr. Griffin seemed to be **appraising** her. "What are you, a sophomore?"

"Junior," Kristen replied **indignantly**.

Dr. Griffin squinted thoughtfully. "Fairfield?" he asked. Kristen's eyes widened in surprise. "Lucky guess," Dr. Griffin said. Then, leaning closer, he added, "Actually, she sends a lot of business my way."

"But I'm not here to see you," Kristen reminded him.

"Not today," he replied with a shrug. Kristen was about to tell him *not ever*, when she heard **bickering** whispers in the short hallway outside Dr. Griffin's room.

"Your parents, I **presume**," Dr. Griffin said, nodding toward the door, and within five seconds Kristen's mother and father were standing right there—framed by wood paneling, green shag carpet, and a cloudy blue ceiling and looking none too happy about it.

---

assessing: estimating
qualifications: fitness or eligibility
skirmish: fight

appraising: evaluating
indignantly: resentfully or angrily

bickering: arguing
presume: assume

"As Mrs. Friedman mentioned on the phone, you've been called in because Kristen has been given a three-day suspension from school," Mrs. Miller said. Kristen fixed her attention on one of the lily pads in the Monet print hanging behind her principal's desk, but even with her focus straight ahead, she could feel her parents' stares burning into her temples.

"The reason for the suspension," Mrs. Miller continued, "is that your daughter displayed **aggression** toward a teacher during one of her classes and had to be asked to leave."

"Aggression?" Mr. Carmichael said, his eyes darting from Kristen to the principal and back again. "Did you *hit* a teacher?" he demanded.

Kristen clicked her tongue. "No, of course not." Leave it to her dad to assume the worst.

"Well, then, what happened?" her mother asked. Kristen considered **invoking** her fifth amendment right, to avoid **self-incrimination**, but instead she just rolled her eyes. Mrs. Miller was the one with all the **jargon**—let her explain what she meant by *aggression*. Ms. Graham turned to Mrs. Miller and raised her eyebrows in a silent demand for **elucidation**.

"Kristen directed an **obscenity** at—"

"*Wench* is *not* an obscenity," Kristen **objected**.

"You called a teacher a *wench*?" her mother asked. Kristen rolled her eyes again. She didn't expect them to understand.

"She did," Mrs. Miller said. "In the middle of class, in front of all the other students, creating quite an **uproar**."

---

aggression: hostility
invoking: appealing to
self-incrimination: accusing oneself

jargon: words or terminology
elucidation: clarification
obscenity: curse or profanity

objected: protested
uproar: commotion

"Oh, please," Kristen muttered. *Uproar?* It was probably the first time all year that everyone in the room had actually been paying attention. Ms. Graham shot Kristen a warning look just as Mr. Carmichael leaned forward.

"Forgive me, Mrs. Miller. I don't mean to be **disrespectful**," he began, "but . . . is that *all?* I mean, does calling someone a wench really warrant a suspension? Why not a detention or some other— lesser—form of punishment?" Kristen glanced sideways at her father. Was he actually questioning the high school principal on her behalf? She hadn't thought he had it in him.

Mrs. Miller took a deep breath, drawing herself up to her full seated height, and smiled at Kristen's father with a hint of **condescension**. "I realize, Mr. Carmichael, that it may not sound like a **grave** offense to you, but we simply can't allow students to disrespect their teachers with **impunity**."

"Oh, don't misunderstand me, Mrs. Miller—I'm not suggesting that no punishment is necessary," Mr. Carmichael replied. "I'm simply wondering if perhaps a suspension is a bit, well, **excessive** in this case." Kristen's mother tilted her head and gave a slight nod. She seemed to be wondering the same thing. But Mrs. Miller didn't appear **deterred**.

She flipped open a folder on her desk and removed a form, handing it to Mr. Carmichael. "As you can see," she stated, after giving him a moment to look it over and hand it on to Kristen's mother, "this is not the first **incident** Ms. Fairfield has had with your daughter." Kristen darted her eyes toward the paper and saw that it was a copy of the detention form her mother had signed just last week.

"You didn't tell me about this," Mr. Carmichael said accusingly to his ex-wife.

"It slipped my mind," Kristen's mother said. "Besides—it wasn't for **behavioral** reasons. It was for not completing homework,

---

disrespectful: rude
condescension: contempt
grave: serious
impunity: without punishment

excessive: extreme
deterred: dissuaded or discouraged
incident: occurrence

behavioral: related to how one acts

which, as I understand, Kristen did complete during the detention. It didn't seem like a big deal."

"Well, I'm afraid Ms. Fairfield **erred** by **omitting** a particular detail from that form," Mrs. Miller said, clasping her hands together on her desk. Both of Kristen's parents sat at attention.

"And what might that be?" Ms. Graham asked.

"It seems that when Kristen was unable to correctly answer a question about the previous night's reading, she chose to make an **inappropriate** comment instead—something about a dog urinating on the floor?" she added, looking down her nose at Kristen. Kristen's parents exchanged **bewildered** glances.

"It was *Macbeth*," Kristen huffed. "She asked why Lady Macbeth said, 'Out, damned spot,' and I said it was because the dog peed on the carpet."

Mr. Carmichael brought his hand to his mouth and coughed, and Kristen thought for a second that she caught a **glimpse** of a smile. But if it had been there at all, there was no trace of it left when he brought his hand down.

"So as you can see, Kristen's aggression toward her English teacher has been **escalating** over the last few days—a trend that we do not wish to take lightly. And the detention she was issued last Monday seems to have been **ineffectual**." Mrs. Miller paused for a moment to let this point sink in. "I'm interested to know," she went on finally, "whether you've been experiencing any difficulty with Kristen at home."

Mr. Carmichael chuckled. "Show me a parent with a teenager who hasn't experienced some difficulty," he said, attempting to **inject** a bit of humor, but Ms. Graham wasn't laughing.

"Well, there was that incident with the police Friday night," Kristen's mom said, glancing **sheepishly** at Mrs. Miller.

"The police?" Mr. Carmichael exclaimed. "What on earth are you talking about?"

---

erred: blundered
omitting: excluding or disregarding
inappropriate: unsuitable

bewildered: puzzled
glimpse: momentary view or hint
escalating: increasing

ineffectual: futile
inject: introduce
sheepishly: timidly

"Didn't you get my message?" Ms. Graham asked.

"Message? What message?"

"I left a message on your machine Saturday morning telling you that your daughter had been brought home by the police and asking you to call me back," Kristen's mother said, her voice low and **staccato**.

"I never got it," Mr. Carmichael said. "I stayed at Carrie's this weekend and went to work from there this morning. Why didn't you call my cell?"

"Because I'm not responsible for getting your messages to you," Kristen's mother barked. "I'm not your secretary, Steven—she's the one you're sleeping with."

Kristen sat up, stunned by the **resentment** in her mother's voice. She'd heard her mother **upbraid** her father before—that was nothing new. But that note in her voice when she'd mentioned Carrie . . . she sounded pretty angry.

"Mr. and Mrs. Carmichael—"

"It's *Graham*," Kristen's mother corrected quickly.

"I'm sorry. But let's try to remain focused on Kristen. Now what were you saying about the police?"

Kristen slumped back in her chair again while her mother **relayed** the events of Friday night, including the facts that Kristen had admitted she'd been drinking and that she was being punished appropriately.

"I intended to discuss it with you when you called back, Steven, and I certainly would have tried phoning you again if I hadn't heard from you by tonight," Ms. Graham added hastily.

"Well, I'm afraid this **complicates** things further," Mrs. Miller said when Kristen's mother had finished.

"What do you mean?" Ms. Graham asked.

"Your daughter has been engaging in risky behavior, Mrs. Graham—"

---

staccato: disjointed	**upbraid:** scold	**complicates:** confuses
resentment: indignation	**relayed:** communicated or transmitted	

"*Ms.* Graham," Kristen's mother interrupted, her voice rising. "It's *Ms.*"

Kristen, her father, and Mrs. Miller all stared at Kristen's mother.

"I guess we all know where Kristen gets her **temperament**," Mr. Carmichael muttered.

"*Steven,*" she replied, warningly. Then, looking to Mrs. Miller, she added, "I'm sorry. It's been a long day. Please go on."

Mrs. Miller cleared her throat. "As I was saying, it appears that Kristen has not only been increasingly hostile in school, she has been engaging in risky behavior outside of school, as well. It seems to me that your daughter might have some serious anger issues that really should be addressed. Therefore, I would like to recommend that she meet with our school psychologist, Dr. Griffin."

"A *psychologist?*" Mr. Carmichael said. "Do you really think that's necessary?"

Mrs. Miller shrugged. "Perhaps not," she admitted. "But I'd rather be safe than sorry, wouldn't you?"

Kristen scoffed. How were her parents supposed to answer that? *No, we'd prefer to be **negligent** and assume everything will turn out fine. After all, she doesn't have access to firearms—at least, not that we know of.*

"I . . . guess so," Ms. Graham said, eyeing her ex-husband.

"Yes . . . certainly," he agreed.

Predictable, Kristen thought, shaking her head. If they only knew that they'd just secured her an appointment with a tie-dye-wearing, ponytailed hippie wanna-be who worked out of a storage closet. Maybe then they would have answered differently.

---

temperament: disposition   **negligent:** careless or neglectful   **predictable:** foreseeable

"Back so soon?" Dr. Griffin said, settling himself into the orange chair **opposite** Kristen.

She scowled. "Not by choice," she replied.

"Yeah, that's the problem with being a school psychologist," Dr. Griffin said. "Very few students actually choose to come see me on their own." He crossed one leg over the other, his left ankle resting on his right knee, and Kristen saw that he was wearing two different-colored socks—one blue and one black. She stared at his feet, stone-faced. Students would have to be completely out of their minds to come to him of their own **volition**—he was a freak. If she actually thought she needed psychological help—which she didn't—she certainly wouldn't seek it from a middle-aged man who couldn't even **coordinate** his own footwear.

Dr. Griffin opened a folder on his lap and thumbed through a couple of papers. "So what did you call Ms. Fairfield, anyway? It just says 'rude name' here. I'd love to hear the details." Kristen remained silent, but Dr. Griffin seemed **unfazed**. "Ah well, doesn't really matter," he said. "She's been called pretty much everything. I guess the real question is why. You want to tell me about that?"

Kristen shrugged.

Dr. Griffin sat back in his seat, closed the folder, and watched her for a minute. "I can tell you right away that if you've somehow gone **mute** between when I saw you just over an hour ago and now, then I'm definitely going to have to recommend **intensive** therapy—either with me or another psychologist. If, however, your **taciturnity** is due to the fact that you think talking with me is a complete waste of your time, I would encourage you to say something to con-

---

opposite: facing or across from

volition: choice or will

coordinate: synchronize

unfazed: undaunted

mute: silent

intensive: rigorous

taciturnity: silence

vince me that that's the case. If you do, then you could walk out of here this afternoon and never have to lay eyes on this **ludicrous** green carpet again." He steepled his fingertips together in front of his face. "If you don't, you might find yourself spending a bit of time in this room."

Kristen watched his hands—two spiders doing push-ups—and **ruminated** over what he had said. "What do I need to say?" she asked.

"Whatever you want to say."

Kristen sighed. *Big help.* "About what?"

"I don't know," Dr. Griffin said. "How about starting with Ms. Fairfield? Did she piss you off?"

"Yes."

"How?"

"She was being really rude," Kristen said. "She asked me a question and I got it right, and she acted like it was some kind of miracle."

"Does she think you're stupid?"

"She thinks everyone is stupid," Kristen said.

"But we're not talking about everyone," Dr. Griffin replied. "We're talking about you. Does she think you're stupid?"

Kristen shrugged. "Probably," she said, "but I don't care. I don't have **self-esteem** problems or anything, if that's what you're thinking. I didn't call her a wench because she hurt my feelings."

"Ah, so it was *wench*," Dr. Griffin said with a smile. "Nice choice. *Witch* is kind of **feeble**, and *bitch* is **unimaginative** and overused." Kristen raised her eyebrows. If he thought he was going to connect with her by talking like a teenager, he had another thing coming. "Why did you call her a wench, then, if it wasn't because she upset you?"

---

ludicrous: absurd
ruminated: pondered
self-esteem: self-respect
feeble: weak
unimaginative: dull

"I didn't say she didn't upset me," Kristen corrected him. "I just said she didn't hurt my feelings. I *was* angry—she was being a wench."

"So you called her one?"

"Yeah."

"Sounds simple enough," Dr. Griffin said. "But Mrs. Miller seems to think you have anger issues. She wrote here that you seem **volatile**. What do you think about that?"

"I think Mrs. Miller needs a little more fun in her life," Kristen muttered.

"Perhaps we should share that thought with Mr. Miller," Dr. Griffin suggested. "But, Mrs. Miller's **personal** life aside, what do you think about this anger thing? Do you feel **irate** a lot of the time? Do you think maybe you do have anger issues?"

"No more than anyone else," Kristen said.

"Unfortunately, that's not saying much," Dr. Griffin replied. "There are a lot of unhealthy people in this world. Fitting in doesn't necessarily make you a picture of mental health. It's kind of like being the most **robust** person in a nursing home—it doesn't mean you're ready to run a marathon."

Kristen cocked her head. Were therapists supposed to say stuff like that? This guy definitely seemed a little **unorthodox**. "So what, then? You think everyone should be in therapy?"

"**Frequent** mental checkups wouldn't hurt," Dr. Griffin said. "But let's get back to you. How did your parents handle the meeting with Mrs. Miller?"

"The way they handle everything," Kristen said.

"And how's that?"

"Poorly."

Dr. Griffin leaned forward. "What do you mean? Did they blow up at you?"

"Not really."

---

volatile: explosive
personal: private
irate: angry

robust: healthy
unorthodox: nonconformist
or unusual

frequent: regular

"Then what did they do poorly?"

Kristen uncrossed her legs and recrossed them in the other direction. "I don't know. They just . . . well, for one thing, they argue. Constantly."

"Mr. and Mrs. Bickerson, huh?"

"Yeah. At least they used to be. They're di—" Kristen stopped, realizing that she'd begun to **divulge** information voluntarily. "They're divorced now," she finished, pressing her lips together.

"Everything you say to me is **confidential**," he assured her.

"Don't you have to tell some of it to my parents and Mrs. Miller?"

Dr. Griffin shook his head. "Nope. I just have to tell them if I think you need to see someone or not."

"Do I?"

"I'm not sure yet. Tell me more about your parents—what were they bickering about?"

"I don't know," Kristen said with a shrug.

"Try to remember. Nothing you say leaves this room, and the truth could set you free," Dr. Griffin **coaxed**.

Kristen chewed on the inside of her cheek and thought back to the meeting. "My dad was mad because my mom didn't tell him about the detention I got last week—or the **episode** with the police. And my mom was mad because he spent the weekend at his girlfriend's and never bothered to check his messages."

"Was that it?" Dr. Griffin asked.

"I think so," Kristen said. "Except that my mom nearly took Mrs. Miller's head off when she called her *Mrs.* Graham instead of *Ms.* Graham."

"So they didn't really argue about *you* or your situation."

"No, but that's no surprise," Kristen said. "They're always more concerned about how stuff **affects** *them*. Like the other night, when the police brought me home—my mom went on and on about how

---

divulge: reveal   **coaxed:** urged   **affects:** influences or upsets
confidential: private   **episode:** occurrence

embarrassing it was for her and how I could have put her job in **jeopardy**."

"Why did the police bring you home?" Dr. Griffin asked.

Kristen winced. She was such an idiot—she'd totally fallen for his routine. She was probably officially screwed now. "Because I'd been drinking," Kristen said. It was easier than a lie at that point.

"And . . . did you call them because you couldn't drive, or did they pick you up somewhere? How did you end up with the police?"

"I was walking home from a party and a cruiser happened to come by."

"And the officer picked you up . . . why? Because you were stumbling and falling down?"

Kristen shook her head. "No, I wasn't even drunk. I hadn't had anything to drink for a while."

"So then . . . I'm confused. Why did the officer pick you up?"

"He wanted to make sure I got home safely," Kristen said. "It was cold and—"

"How cold?"

"I don't know—twenty-something?" Kristen guessed. Dr. Griffin nodded. "And I had a long way to go—"

"How far?"

Kristen rolled her eyes. "He said it was something like ten miles, but I don't—"

"You **undertook** a ten-mile walk in twenty-degree weather?" Dr. Griffin asked. "At what time of night?"

"One-thirty, two—something like that," Kristen mumbled.

"But didn't you say you'd been at a party?" Dr. Griffin asked.

"Yes."

"With other people?"

"Ye-es," Kristen said. What was this guy—a complete dork? Without other people, it wouldn't have been a party.

---

jeopardy: danger   undertook: attempted

"So then why were you walking home alone in twenty-degree weather? Did you walk there?"

"No."

"What happened to your ride?"

Kristen clenched her hands, looking down at the floor. She didn't really want to go into the **sordid** details of Luke's party and its subsequent **impact** on her social life. She was doing everything she could to force the image of Trevor pushing up against her out of her mind.

"Kristen? What are you leaving out here?"

Kristen groaned. "Look, I really don't want to get into this right now."

"You don't have to go into detail," Dr. Griffin said. "I'm just wondering why you would choose to walk ten miles in the cold instead of going home with a friend or spending the night or—"

"Oh, yeah, right," Kristen exclaimed. "That would have been good. Then the rumors would have been even better."

"Better than what?" Dr. Griffin asked.

Kristen felt the water beginning to well up in her eyes and blinked **rapidly** to keep it under control. She struggled to maintain her **stolid** expression. "Are there rumors going around right now?" Dr. Griffin asked.

Kristen bit her lip and willed the tears away. Even so, Dr. Griffin grabbed a box of tissues that had been stashed on the floor next to his chair and set them on the coffee table in front of her. "I want to remind you one more time that anything you say in here is absolutely confidential," he said.

"I don't want to talk about it," Kristen said. Her voice was shaky, but she'd managed to **banish** the moisture from her eyes.

"Okay," Dr. Griffin said. "You don't have to tell me. But what do your friends say about these rumors?"

---

sordid: wretched or dirty   **rapidly:** quickly   **banish:** remove or dismiss
impact: effect   **stolid:** impassive

Kristen laughed **cynically**. "I don't *have* any friends," she said. "Are we almost done here?"

Dr. Griffin nodded. "Yeah, I think we're done," he said. "But I am going to recommend that you come back again."

"Why?" Kristen said. "I'm not some head case, you know. I just need everyone to leave me alone."

"I don't think you're a head case," Dr. Griffin said.

"But you think I have *anger issues*?" Kristen sneered.

"I'm not sure they're anger issues, **per se**," Dr. Griffin replied. "But it does seem to me that you lack connectivity."

"What's that supposed to mean?"

"It means that you don't seem particularly connected at home, and you don't seem particularly connected at school. Would you say that's true?"

"Connected to what?" Kristen snapped.

"To other people, pets, an organization, a cause—something outside of yourself that connects you to the world. Would you say that's true?"

Kristen thought about surfing—how she felt on her board when she was riding a wave, how the ocean **alleviated** her pain, how she could go in feeling the weight of the world on her shoulders and come out feeling like she was flying. Surely surfing was something that connected her to the world. But she'd already told Dr. Griffin too much about her life, and surfing wasn't something she wanted to share.

"I guess," she said.

"You **hesitated**," Dr. Griffin pointed out. "Is there someone you feel close to, Kristen? Someone you can really share yourself with? Someone you trust?"

Kristen shook her head. "No," she admitted. The ocean certainly didn't **qualify** as a person—the ocean was way better than that.

---

cynically: skeptically
per se: intrinsically or basically

alleviated: relieved

hesitated: wavered
qualify: fit

"Well, that's why I'd like to see you again. People without connectivity **tend** to be at a higher risk for problems like depression—"

"I'm not depressed," Kristen said.

"I didn't say you were. I just said that people who aren't connected tend to be at a higher risk for such things, and I'd like to make sure that you're not headed down that path."

"So . . . what do I have to do? Meet with you once a week or something?" Kristen asked.

"Actually, I'd like you to meet with me as part of a group that I run."

Kristen narrowed her eyes. "What kind of group?"

"Just a group of students in **similar circumstances**. We meet every Tuesday afternoon during period five, and we talk about whatever's on people's minds. Sometimes we discuss issues, sometimes I run activities—it varies. But the point of the group is to support each other and provide an outlet for kids who are having issues in school or at home—"

"I'm not having issues," Kristen protested.

"_Or,_" Dr. Griffin went on, "kids who aren't particularly connected anywhere else. So, what do you say?"

"Do I have a choice?" Kristen asked.

"You always have a choice," Dr. Griffin said. "But keep in mind that if you agree to attend the group, I can have your suspension **waived** so that you can start right in tomorrow. And of course, if you decide not to attend, you're the one who'll have to explain to your parents why you chose the suspension over the support group."

Kristen took a deep breath. There wasn't much room to **vacillate**. If her parents knew she could have gotten out of the suspension and she'd chosen not to, they'd kill her. They'd already had a twenty-minute discussion about how **impracticable** it was going to be for them supervise her over the next three days with their busy schedules.

---

tend: are likely
similar: comparable
circumstances: situations

waived: dismissed or postponed
vacillate: hesitate or fluctuate

impracticable: difficult or impossible

"Fine. I'll do it," she said, recognizing that joining Dr. Griffin's **asinine** group was probably the easiest way for her to avoid **censure**. After all, her parents couldn't give her too much grief if she had serious issues, could they? They'd have to be completely **merciless** to **persecute** someone with bona fide emotional problems. And besides, period five was English with Ms. Fairfield. Missing that class once a week wouldn't exactly break her heart.

---

asinine: stupid   **merciless:** pitiless   **persecute:** victimize
censure: criticism

By the time Kristen reached Dr. Griffin's room the next day at the start of period five, the two orange chairs and the sofa were occupied. True, she could have sat at the center of the couch—only the end cushions were taken—but to do so, she would have had to squeeze between Ellen Stank, whom Tracy referred to as Smellin' Stank because the name sort of fit her, and Alice Tartan, whom Tracy called Alice *Titan* because of her size.

Kristen had always been grateful that her name was difficult to **ridicule** and rhyme. Of course, Tracy was bound to come up with an **unflattering pseudonym** for her sooner or later, but at least Kristen's parents hadn't made it an easy task by giving her a **moniker** that lent itself to such **denigration**.

Still, even as she sympathized with Ellen and Alice over their unfortunate **aliases**, Kristen had no desire to bond with them by sharing a piece of furniture. Instead, she selected a red beanbag chair and plopped herself into it, sinking a little farther back than she had **anticipated** and nearly knocking her head on the floor, **eliciting diffident** smirks from a few of the regulars.

"I love those things, but there is definitely an art to sitting in them," Dr. Griffin said as Kristen worked to **rectify** her posture. She **glowered** in his general direction. Thanks to his comment, everyone in the room was now staring at her, including Ellen, Alice, and Macy Ames, the pregnant girl who was occupying the orange chair across from Dr. Griffin's.

Macy was a junior who had been **virtually** unknown prior to her pregnancy, but now everyone knew who she was, whether they knew her name or not. She had been **dubbed** "the pregnant girl" a

titan: giant	**denigration:** vilification or slander	**diffident:** distrustful
ridicule: mock or tease		**rectify:** correct
unflattering: unfavorable	**aliases:** false names or pseudonyms	**glowered:** scowled
pseudonym: false name or alias		**virtually:** nearly
moniker: name	**anticipated:** expected	**dubbed:** named
	eliciting: evoking	

good month ago when it had become **evident** that she wasn't simply putting on weight—she was putting on baby.

"It looks like just about everyone is here," Dr. Griffin said, glancing around. "So let's get started." Unlike in other classes, no one was chatting while waiting for class to start, so Dr. Griffin only had to make his request once to have everyone sitting quietly and paying attention—or at least appearing to pay attention.

"As I'm sure you've all noticed," he went on, "we have a new member today, so I'd like to start by going over the group rules, okay?" There seemed to be **general** agreement in the room, although no one actually nodded or spoke.

"Okay. The first rule of Fight Club is you do not talk about Fight Club," Dr. Griffin said. Kristen scrunched up her eyebrows. She was just beginning to wonder what she'd gotten herself into when Dr. Griffin's **sober** expression **dissolved** into a smile.

"I'm just kidding, Kristen," Dr. Griffin said. "Did you ever see the movie *Fight Club*? Brad Pitt, Edward Norton?"

"Nope." Leah and Tracy had tried to get her to come over when they'd rented it once, so they could all drool over Brad together, but Kristen had chosen an afternoon of surfing instead.

"Ah, well. Mikey here," Dr. Griffin said, pointing to the small redhead on his left who occupied a multicolored patchwork beanbag chair, "mentioned one day that our first rule is a lot like their first rule, so sometimes we like to make a little joke about it." Kristen looked around the room. *Some joke.* Nobody seemed to be laughing. Then again, this wasn't exactly a gathering of well-adjusted, happy-go-lucky **adolescents**. *I* so *do not belong here*, Kristen thought. Granted, she hadn't been doing very well on the friend front lately, but these kids were completely lacking in social skills.

"Our real first rule is . . . anybody?"

There was a pause as he gazed around at everyone, waiting for someone to finish the sentence. Finally Macy raised her head

---

evident: obvious   **sober:** serious   **adolescents:** teenagers
general: extensive or   **dissolved:** melted
popular

slightly. "Anything said in this room stays in this room," she said quietly.

"That's correct," Dr. Griffin said, returning his focus to Kristen. "We talk about a lot of serious issues here, and a lot of personal issues. And in order for this to be a safe environment for those types of discussions, we all need to **adhere** to a strict code of confidentiality. How about rule number two?"

This question was greeted by complete silence, lasting longer than before.

Kristen watched as Dr. Griffin looked from face to face, and one student after another **averted** his or her eyes, finding something **captivating** to **observe** on the floor, on the ceiling—anywhere but in Dr. Griffin's line of sight. It was the classic don't-call-on-me move, but Kristen couldn't help thinking that these kids took it to another level. The tension in the room was **palpable**, and most of them looked as though they would die of **mortification** if anyone actually asked them for an answer.

I really don't belong here, Kristen thought.

"Anyone?" Dr. Griffin asked again. Kristen was on the verge of **venturing** a guess when the door opened, sending a wave of relief through the room, the group's long-standing members thankful for the brief **respite** from **scrutiny** they'd been given. And now it was Kristen's turn to be **mortified**.

"Nate—glad you could join us," Dr. Griffin said.

There, dressed completely in black once again, stood Nate Jacobs—the boy who had witnessed Kristen's brief **incarceration** in the back of Officer Doyle's cruiser, thereby giving Tracy and company more **fodder** for their rumor mill. Kristen glared at him, and then, almost as if he had felt her stare, Nate turned and looked directly at her with his moody, dark brown eyes.

He held Kristen's gaze for a moment then blinked and looked at Dr. Griffin. "Sorry," he said. "Boynton kept me late again." He **prof-**

---

adhere: stick
averted: turned away
captivating: delightful or enchanting
observe: watch or study

palpable: tangible or perceptible
mortification: humiliation or shame
venturing: risking
respite: reprieve or delay

scrutiny: investigation
mortified: ashamed or humiliated
incarceration: imprisonment
fodder: food or material
proffered: offered

fered a small pink slip that Dr. Griffin barely glanced at before tucking into his pocket.

"You can **redeem** yourself right now by answering this question," Dr. Griffin said. "Group rule number one is that anything said in this room stays in this room. What's rule number two?"

Nate smirked. "There is no rule number two," he said.

Dr. Griffin smiled and nodded, and the rest of the group members grinned at Nate.

"Oh, Mr. G., you're such a jerk," Macy said. Kristen was surprised the shy girl had dared such a direct **affront**, but Dr. Griffin just chuckled. Meanwhile, Nate grabbed a beanbag chair in a camouflage pattern and pulled it up next to Macy. Then, **effortlessly**, he settled into it, achieving a perfect **equilibrium** of lower padding and upper support on the first try. Obviously, he had **perfected** the art to which Dr. Griffin had been referring.

"As you can see, Kristen, we're a pretty informal group. Confidentiality is the only thing we **require** of one another. As Nate so **succinctly** put it, *there is no rule number two.*"

"Yeah, but there *is* something else you gotta be in here," Mikey said. Again, Kristen was surprised to hear someone in the group speak out in a less than **timorous** voice. But as she looked around, she realized that something had changed since Nate had walked in. Postures had relaxed and faces had become more **animated**. Of course, it could have been Macy's comment that had loosened them up, but even Macy had seemed somewhat **discomfited** until Nate had arrived.

"And what's that, Mikey?" Dr. Griffin asked.

"Honest," the redhead answered, eyeing Kristen. "So what's Miss Popularity doing here?" he asked. "Writing an article on us for the school newspaper?"

Everyone stared at Kristen until she felt like a pair of lacy thong underwear hung out to dry in a public park.

---

redeem: save	**perfected:** refined	**animated:** lively
affront: insult	**require:** demand or ask	**discomfited:** flustered
effortlessly: easily	**succinctly:** concisely	
equilibrium: balance	**timorous:** fearful	

"Whoa, Mikey—why don't you introduce yourself to our new member before you start attacking her," Dr. Griffin suggested. "Kristen, this is Mikey. Mikey, this is Kristen. And no, she is not here to write an article about you for the school newspaper or *Rolling Stone* or the *Enquirer*—sorry to disappoint you."

There were a few chortles from Ellen and Alice, but Mikey continued to stare **askance** at Kristen. "Then why is she here?" he asked.

"That's for Kristen to reveal in her own time," Dr. Griffin said.

"Probably because of all the rumors," a girl Kristen had barely noticed before interjected.

"What rumors?" Mikey asked.

"All right everyone, let's not—," Dr. Griffin began, but he was too late.

"Haven't you heard?" the girl said. "Little Miss Perfect gets around—a little too much for her rich-bitch friends. The other weekend she—"

"Okay, that's enough," Dr. Griffin said. "Honesty is important, Mikey, but so is respect. We don't badger people in this group, and we don't spread rumors. And you, Lindsey, owe a quarter to the insult jar," he added.

Lindsey's mouth fell open, and Kristen noticed she had a silver bolt through the center of her tongue. Of course that was no surprise, considering she also had piercings in her nose and one eyebrow, along with about seven black hoops hanging from each ear. With her spiky blue-black hair and dark eye makeup, Kristen couldn't help thinking that the name Lindsey was a bit too delicate for her. Lilith would have been more **apt**.

Only five minutes into the group, Kristen was feeling a bit raw from having already been **assailed**, but something Dr. Griffin had just said struck a chord within her. She cleared her throat. "Um, did you say that you don't spread rumors in this group?" she asked.

"I did," Dr. Griffin **affirmed** with a nod.

---

askance: scornfully or disapprovingly

apt: likely
assailed: attacked

affirmed: asserted

"Well then, I'd like to know why *he* told everybody that he saw me in a police car last Friday night," she said, doing her best to stare down Nate for having **contributed** to her misery. Unfortunately, he didn't appear the least bit **ruffled** by either her accusation or her **menacing** gaze. On the contrary—he laughed.

"Me?" he asked, **incredulous**.

"Yes, you," Kristen snapped.

Nate looked at her with a combination of **contempt** and pity. "Believe it or not, you're not one of my **primary** topics of conversation," he said.

"Well, if it wasn't you, who was it?" Kristen demanded. "You're the only one who saw me in that car."

Someone coughed, and Kristen turned to see Alice looking at her sheepishly. "No, he isn't," she said, her voice barely above a whisper.

Kristen blinked. "What are you talking about?"

Alice darted a look at Dr. Griffin, who nodded. "It's okay, Alice," he said. "We're all **bound** by confidentiality here. If you know something that might help Kristen sort out her anger with Nate, it could be helpful."

Oh for God's sake, Kristen thought. This guy was so New Age-y it was pathetic. Still, she tried to keep her **disdain** to herself. If Alice really did have something to say, she wanted to hear it. But from the way Alice was **avoiding** eye contact, full **disclosure** didn't seem likely.

Kristen tried to wait, but her patience was **dwindling**. "Did *you* see me?" she asked finally.

"Yes," Alice said, her chin down so that it looked like she was speaking to her own chest.

"You were there, at the station? I didn't see you anywhere around."

---

contributed: given or added	**contempt:** disgust or disdain	**avoiding:** evading
ruffled: agitated	**primary:** main	**disclosure:** revelation
menacing: threatening	**bound:** restricted	**dwindling:** shrinking or
incredulous: disbelieving	**disdain:** scorn	decreasing

"No, I wasn't there," Alice explained. "But I saw you get dropped off at home, by the cop. I live at Riverside too," she added, referring to the complex of town houses where Kristen's mom had bought a place after the divorce. "A lot of kids from school do, actually—including Josh Bank, on the football team. I'm pretty sure he saw too, and he was the one who told everyone."

Kristen's jaw went slack. It hadn't even occurred to her that someone might have seen her arrive home by police escort, even though she knew there were other students who lived around her—some of them rode the same bus as her and got off at her stop. True, Officer Doyle hadn't used his flashing lights, but it was a well-lit street, and a police car driving through at 2 A.M., when there was little other traffic around, would certainly have stood out to anyone who had been awake.

"Oh," she said. She looked around the room at all the disapproving stares, realizing that in her first ten minutes with these kids, she'd managed to insult their leader with a false accusation and **estrange** herself from everyone. She seemed to have a real **knack** for doing that lately.

She glanced at Nate, who was watching her **expectantly**. "Sorry," she muttered in Nate's direction, feeling like a jerk for having **broached** the subject at all. She should have known it couldn't have been him. None of her friends would have taken any claims he'd made seriously. And, like he'd said, she wasn't exactly his primary topic of conversation.

"No problem," Nate said. "I'm used to it."

"He wears a lot of black," Macy put in. "He gets accused of a lot of things." At that, Nate actually chuckled, his typically **somber** expression softening into one that was almost **ebullient**. Kristen was surprised by how completely the simple act of laughing **transformed** his face. Between his wide smile, deep dimples, and the

---

estrange: alienate
knack: talent
expectantly: anxiously or hopefully

broached: introduced
somber: gloomy

ebullient: ecstatic or exuberant
transformed: changed

smooth lines at the outsides of his eyes, he actually appeared **affable**. And, Kristen couldn't help noticing, kind of cute.

It wasn't until he glanced back at her that Kristen realized she had been staring. Swallowing hard, she began to examine the freckle on her left thumb closely, as if discovering it for the first time. And while she pretended to scrutinize the small dot that had been with her since birth, she remained **acutely** aware of the fact that Nate was now staring at her with a gaze that seemed to be melting her insides and **generating** goosebumps on her flesh at the same time.

Well, whatever. So he was cute—he was still Nate Jacobs, which meant he inhabited a whole different social world from her. She'd go to this group if it meant keeping her parents off her back, but she didn't need to get any of Dr. Griffin's "connectivity" from people like them.

---

affable: friendly   **acutely:** intensely   **generating:** producing

"D'accord—maintenant il est temps de finir vos pieces, et puis les practiquer, s'il vous plait. Nous les exécuterons demain."

Chairs scraped the industrial-grade tile floor as students rearranged themselves into small groups at Madame de Gaulle's request. Between the dull buzz of voices and the metallic grating of desk legs against vinyl, it sounded like a herd of cattle with **sinus** infections had **meandered** into the room.

Reluctantly, Kristen pulled her chair over to join her group, which **consisted** of Jill Enders, Michelle Spencer, and Leah. They'd formed the groups in the week before Luke's party, and, recognizing that Leah and Kristen were friends, Mme de Gaulle had placed them in a group together. She'd avoided adding Tracy and Stephanie to the mix, however, knowing all too well that groups made up entirely of close friends were **seldom** productive. So Tracy and Stephanie were across the room in a group with Alec Bartley and Cynthia Perkins, and for that, at least, Kristen was thankful. Being in a group with Leah, however, was proving to be no picnic, either.

Leah hadn't spoken to Kristen—not even a quick hello in the hallway—since Monday's exchange, and she'd been avoiding making eye contact too. Either she believed all of the rumors and was thoroughly disgusted with Kristen's **alleged** behavior, or she had simply decided it was wise to steer clear of the object of Tracy's **scorn** for fear of being found guilty by association. Whatever her reasons for **eschewing** her former best friend, Kristen wasn't impressed. She'd expected a little more loyalty from someone she'd known since she was six. But then, she'd expected her parents to

---

sinus: nasal	**seldom:** rarely	**scorn:** contempt
meandered: wandered	**alleged:** supposed	**eschewing:** avoiding
consisted: included		

stay together and Uncle Pete to always be around, and a million other things that hadn't happened either. It seemed that the only thing she could count on lately was being let down. She hadn't even been able to get in her Wednesday morning surfing because of her stupid grounding, which her parents had agreed would include absolutely no surfing for two weeks.

"Okay, we need to finish this skit," Jill said. "I think—"

"En francais, s'il vous plait," Mme de Gaulle **intoned** as she **strolled** by.

Jill sighed. *"D'accord."* She began again, in French as the teacher had requested. *"Je pense qu'il serait amusant si nous. . . ."*

Kristen zoned out as Jill spoke, focusing instead on Tracy's voice about ten feet behind her.

"How do you spell *whore* in French?" she was asking the members of her group, but before anyone could answer, she said, "Oh wait—I know. It's K-R-I-S-T-E-N, right?" This was, of course, followed by snickering and Mme de Gaulle's question, *"Qu'est-ce qu'il se passe?"*

"Nothing, I mean, *rien*, Madame de Gaulle," Tracy said. Kristen bit the inside of her cheek and returned her attention to her group, only to find that they too must have heard Tracy's comment. Michelle and Jill were looking down at their desks, smirking, and Leah wouldn't meet her eye.

It was only second period, and already Kristen could tell it was going to be a long day.

*   *   *   *   *

"Three-fifty," the cashier said to Kristen at the end of the lunch line. Kristen glanced down at the spaghetti on her tray, the single piece of garlic bread, and the sixteen-ounce bottle of Poland Spring water she'd selected and decided that school lunches were getting way too

---

intoned: uttered   **strolled:** walked

expensive. How was she supposed to save money if lunch for the week used up the entire twenty bucks her mother gave her each Monday for the **intended** purpose. It used to be that she could get by spending just five or ten and saving the **surplus** for surf gear and **accessories**. But now, with even the most basic lunch costing three-fifty, she was going to have to come up with a new strategy.

And, she realized, as she accepted her change from the cafeteria lady, she was going to have to come up with a new strategy for finding a seat too.

Standing in front of the cash register and off to the side to avoid blocking traffic, Kristen gazed around the **enormous** room filled with round tables surrounded by metal and plastic chairs. Yesterday she'd chanced sitting with Stephanie, since Leah and Tracy weren't there yet, but Stephanie had blatantly ignored her, sending the message loud and clear—Kristen was not wanted at their usual table.

So when a group of sophomores **vacated** a table in the back corner, Kristen jumped on it. Of course, sitting alone wasn't much better than sitting with someone who ignored her. At least yesterday she'd had the **consolation** that she hadn't stood out particularly. Today, on the other hand, she was the only person sitting at a table for eight.

Even worse, no one showed any interest in joining her—not even the freshman and sophomore boys who used to flirt with her **incessantly** when she was out with Tracy, Steph, and Leah getting pizza or ice cream or just **patronizing** the local coffee shop. It was as though she had gone from being part of the high school elite to being a social leper overnight. Now she got why her friends hadn't understood how easily she'd **scorned** popularity when she had it. Maybe a lot of things about her friends had bugged her, but being an outsider was a lot scarier.

Just focus on your food, Kristen told herself. After all, she was there to eat, anyway, not make friends. She'd just wolf down what

---

intended: planned
surplus: extra or leftover
accessories: extras

enormous: huge
vacated: left
consolation: comfort
incessantly: repeatedly

patronizing: supporting
scorned: disdained or dismissed

she needed, then head to her locker to get ready for English. Maybe she'd even get to Fairfield's class early and get some of her homework out of the way. *Oh, man,* Kristen thought, twirling pasta on her fork. She'd been **reduced** to actually concentrating on her schoolwork for lack of anything better to do. How **pitiable** was that?

"Okay if I join you?"

Kristen glanced up to see Macy Ames, the pregnant girl—also known as Preggy Sue, the Incubator, the Oven, she who was **gestationally** challenged—standing next to her table. *Great. Just what I need,* Kristen thought. As if she wasn't being **ostracized** enough.

"Um, can I sit here?" Macy asked, tapping one of the chairs at Kristen's table. Then she looked around the cafeteria. "There aren't exactly a lot of free seats, you know," she added.

"Oh," Kristen said, wishing Macy would just go away. But she didn't. She just stood and waited for an answer. "Um, sure," Kristen said finally. As much as she wanted to say no, she found that she just didn't have it in her.

"Thanks," Macy said. She pulled out a chair and **situated** herself so that she was facing Kristen. "So what did you think of group?" she asked.

Kristen found herself glancing around the cafeteria before she replied, making sure that no one was watching her **interact** with such an **outcast**. "It was okay," she said without making eye contact. If she kept her answers short and never actually met Macy's gaze, maybe Macy would get the hint and leave her alone.

"I heard that you have to be there because you're some kind of sex addict," Macy said, taking a big bite of her salad.

Kristen almost choked on a strand of spaghetti. "You what?" she asked, when she'd finally stopped coughing.

"I thought that might get your attention," Macy said with a smile.

Kristen narrowed her eyes. "What? You mean you made that up?"

---

reduced: limited or restricted **ostracized:** excluded **outcast:** exile or reject
pitiable: contemptible **situated:** placed
gestationally: pregnantly **interact:** cooperate

"No, I heard it," Macy said. "From your friends." She gestured with her fork toward the table where Stephanie and Leah had been joined by Tracy, Luke, Trevor, Michelle, and Jill.

"They're not my friends," Kristen said.

"What a **coincidence**," Macy said, plunking a cherry tomato into her mouth. "They're not mine, either." She picked through her salad with her fork, finding one more cherry tomato, spearing it, and stuffing that one into her mouth as well. "Ever since I hit month five, I've been craving tomatoes like they were Tootsie Rolls. Weird, huh?"

Kristen shrugged. "I guess," she said. She watched as Macy **inhaled** the rest of her salad, downed a pint of milk, and then moved on to her pasta, twirling forkful after forkful into her mouth. After only five minutes, her plate was nearly empty and she was getting ready to move onto dessert. As she grabbed the brownie she'd purchased and began to undo its plastic wrapping, she noticed Kristen's **awed** gaze.

"I know," Macy said, shaking her head. "It's disgusting. I eat like a linebacker. I'm so hungry these days, it's insane. I get back to the house after school and it's like, *feed me!*" She smiled, her blue eyes sparkling. "Luckily, all the other girls there are in the same boat, so they understand."

"The other girls?" Kristen asked.

Macy broke off a piece of her brownie, pushed it into her mouth, and nodded. "I live at Our Choice—it's a shelter for pregnant teens who don't have anywhere else to go."

"You—?"

"Mm-hmm," Macy said. "My aunt couldn't deal with it."

"Your aunt?"

"Yeah. My parents died in a plane crash when I was nine, and I didn't have any other family. It was either Aunt Frida or a foster home, and unfortunately, Aunt Frida came through."

---

coincidence: fluke or chance

inhaled: sucked in

awed: astonished or amazed

"But . . . she kicked you out?" Kristen asked.

"More or less," Macy said. Then she grinned. "She gave me more grief, I wanted less, so I left."

"Wow," Kristen said, setting down her fork. It was almost **unfathomable**. She couldn't imagine being sixteen, pregnant, and on her own, but Macy was practically joking about it—like it was no big deal.

"Yeah, that about sums it up," Macy said. "But it's not as bad as it sounds. The people at the shelter are really supportive, and I'm getting great medical care." She rested her left hand on her belly. "And this little one's getting all the brownies she can eat."

Kristen smiled at Macy's stomach, and then at Macy herself. "It must be weird to be pregnant," she said without thinking. "I mean, not that *you're* weird or anything—"

"Don't bother," Macy said. "I know what you mean, and it is. People stare at me all the time, call me names, laugh at me, spread rumors—but then, you know what that's like."

"Yeah," Kristen said, shifting uncomfortably. Was she really on the same level now as . . . Preggy Sue?

She glanced over at her former friends, who were laughing away, not a care in the world. Probably laughing at her too. "Did you really hear that I was . . . a sex addict?" Kristen whispered, leaning closer to Macy.

Macy paused, winced, and then nodded. "Sorry," she said. "If it's any consolation, I didn't believe it. I didn't believe the stuff about you and Trevor, either. Or the thing about you trying to get Luke and Tracy to be with you at the same time."

Kristen's jaw dropped.

"Ooh—you hadn't heard that one, huh?" Macy asked. Kristen shook her head slowly. What *wasn't* being said about her?

"At least no one's claiming you're pregnant," Macy offered. "That's something, right?"

---

unfathomable:
incomprehensible

Kristen rested her head in her hands. It wasn't exactly the **solace** she was looking for.

"Hey—what are you doing after school today?" Macy asked. Kristen raised her head and met Macy's excited gaze with a **wary** one.

Kristen raised her head, not loving where this was going. "Why?"

"I was just wondering," Macy said. "I thought maybe we could hang out or something."

"Umm," Kristen started, trying to think of a quick excuse. She didn't want to seem **conceited** or anything. Macy actually seemed decent, nicer than Kristen would have thought. But still, hanging out with the pregnant girl wasn't exactly going to help her if she was to have any shot at all of getting past all these disgusting rumors **circulating**. Then she realized she didn't even have to lie. She actually had a **valid** reason not to hang out. "I'm not sure if I can. I'm—"

Macy held up her hand and shook her head. "Don't worry about it," she said. "I just thought I'd ask." She started to gather up her napkin and pile things onto her tray, preparing to leave.

Guilt coursed through Kristen. Macy was the first person she'd encountered who didn't believe all of the rumors, and for that, at least, Kristen felt somewhat **beholden** to her.

"I would," she said, "really. It's just that my mom grounded me and I'm not allowed to do anything. It's just straight to school and straight home, and I have to take the bus, so I can't even make any stops on the way."

Macy paused. "What if I could give you a ride home?" she asked. "Well, actually, I wouldn't be the one giving you a ride—it's Nate's car, but I'm sure he wouldn't mind dropping you off."

"Nate?" Kristen asked. "Nate *Jacobs*?"

"Yeah." Macy nodded. "I know he wouldn't mind, and there's something cool I'd really like to show you."

---

solace: reassurance   **conceited:** self-centered   **valid:** legitimate or sound
wary: cautious   **circulating:** spreading   **beholden:** indebted

Kristen pressed her lips together and tried to weigh the pieces of the **equation**. *Cons: (1) being seen with Macy Ames and Nate Jacobs, (2) **potentially** getting in trouble for not coming straight home (if I get caught), and (3) getting stuck doing something boring that Macy thinks is cool. Pros: (1) doing something other than going home and moping, (2) doing something other than going home and moping, and (3) admit it!—getting a chance to hang out with Nate Jacobs and see what he's about.*

"Forget it," Macy said after Kristen had been silent for a minute or two. "You don't have to." She piled everything onto her tray, grabbed it, and stood up. "Thanks for the seat," she said. Then she turned to go.

"Macy—wait."

Macy stopped and set her tray back on the table. "Yeah?"

"Okay."

Macy scrunched up her eyebrows. "Okay?"

"Yeah. *Okay*," Kristen repeated. "I just have to be home by four-thirty. That's when my mom **typically** calls to check in."

"No problem," Macy said with a grin. "We should be able to get you home by four."

"Cool," Kristen said. Out of the corner of her eye, she noticed that Leah was watching her, but she tried to remain **nonchalant**. If Leah could ignore her, she could certainly return the favor. "So where should I meet you?" she asked, trying to focus all of her attention on Macy.

"At the main entrance to the school at two-thirty," Macy said. "Just be there, and I'll take care of the rest."

"Okay," Kristen said. And as Macy walked away, she willed herself to ignore the laughter coming from Leah's table, difficult though it was. **Indifference** was clearly an emotion she was going to need to **master**.

---

equation: a series of variable factors
potentially: possibly

typically: ordinarily
nonchalant: indifferent or cool

indifference: apathy or disinterest
master: learn

Chapter Eleven

Standing outside the school alone had never been a big deal to Kristen. She was used to hanging out and waiting for her friends to meet her or for her father to pick her up, and in the past, she'd never worried about what anyone passing by might think. But today was different. Today she wasn't Kristen Carmichael, standing alone by choice, bound to be joined by interesting and popular people at any moment. Instead, she was Kristen Carmichael, standing alone because no one wanted anything to do with her, bound to be joined by a pregnant girl who would only draw more negative attention at any moment, and everyone who passed her seemed to be snickering for **precisely** that reason.

Kristen brought her mittened hands to her face and breathed hot air into them to warm her face. Why had she agreed to hang out with Macy and Nate? Macy was pregnant, for God's sake, and Nate was . . . well, not exactly popular, no matter how cute he might look when he managed to actually smile.

When the bus rounded the corner and students began to file on, Kristen found herself **contemplating** boarding herself and just telling Macy she'd spaced on their plans to hang out.

"Ready?"

Kristen jumped. She'd been on the **verge** of taking a step toward the bus when Macy had **materialized** from out of nowhere.

"Sorry—I didn't mean to sneak up on you," Macy said. "In fact, I didn't even think I could sneak up on anyone anymore, I've put on so much weight. Plus I keep misjudging the size of my stomach and bumping into things."

Kristen narrowed her eyes.

---

precisely: exactly   **verge:** brink   **materialized:** appeared
contemplating: considering

"Really," Macy insisted. "The other day I was getting an orange juice at the gas station and I ran right into this big biker dude. I thought I had room to squeeze by, but I forgot about my stomach and I ended up bumping him with my belly."

"What'd he do?" Kristen asked.

"Nothing," Macy said with a shrug. "Just looked at me like he felt sorry for me—the way everyone else does."

"Oh," Kristen said, for lack of anything more **insightful** to say. It couldn't be easy for Macy. She might as well be walking around with a lighted marquee that read, Pregnant Teen or Unwed Mother or Sexually Irresponsible Sixteen-Year-Old in big black letters. Still, she seemed to take it all in **stride**.

"Come on," she said, grabbing Kristen's elbow and urging her forward. "I have to pee."

"Do you want to go back inside the school?" Kristen asked.

"Can't. Nate's waiting," Macy said, and again she gave Kristen a nudge. Realizing that they were headed for the student parking lot, Kristen increased her pace, walking a good ten feet in front of Macy as they crossed in front of the school bus, and lengthening her lead to twenty feet by the time she'd reached the lot—a distance for which she was thankful when she walked in front of Tracy's little red VW Jetta, which was **spewing** exhaust from its tailpipe while it warmed up. Sure, Kristen was hanging out with the pregnant girl, but that didn't mean she had to **advertise** it.

Unfortunately, just as she'd cleared the Tracy zone, she heard Macy calling to her. "Kristen! Back here!" she yelled. Kristen turned to see that Macy was headed toward the other side of the lot.

Great, Kristen thought. But instead of doubling back and walking with Macy, she **opted** to take the long route, **essentially** circling the entire lot to meet up with Macy on the other side.

"What was that about?" Macy asked when they finally crossed paths again at the far end of the parking lot.

---

insightful: perceptive
stride: without difficulty

spewing: discharging or vomiting
advertise: publicize

opted: chose
essentially: necessarily

"What was what about?" Kristen asked, blinking innocently.

Macy scowled. "Forget it," she said. "Just get in." She **gestured** to the bright orange, rust-**corroded** Volvo wagon on her left. Kristen squinted and peered inside. Sure enough, Nate was behind the wheel.

"You can take the front," Macy offered, following her to the passenger side, but Kristen had already **plotted** out a **stratagem** in her mind.

"That's okay—you take it," she said. "You'll be more comfortable there."

"Actually, it doesn't matter," Macy said. "I don't get carsick or anything."

"Yeah, but . . ." Kristen hesitated, trying to come up with a **compelling** reason for Macy to be in front. "This is an old car," she said finally. "It probably just has lap belts in the back, and you should really have the whole shoulder strap thing. Shouldn't you?"

Macy lowered one eyebrow and studied Kristen's face. "I guess," she finally **consented**.

As Kristen reached for the rear door handle, she breathed a silent sigh of relief. It would be much easier to duck down and avoid being spotted in the backseat, and she'd managed to score it without letting Macy know what she was up to. As Kristen settled herself on the striped blanket that stretched across the Volvo's backseat, she felt a certain satisfaction at how well she'd **accomplished** her aim. Unfortunately, Nate didn't seem to share her **enthusiasm**.

"What are you doing here?" he asked, squinting at her in the rearview mirror.

"I invited her," Macy said, scooting into the front seat and pulling down her lap belt. Then she started fidgeting with the controls on the dashboard. "Is the heat on?" she asked.

---

gestured: signaled
corroded: destroyed
plotted: planned
stratagem: trick or ruse

compelling: convincing
consented: agreed
accomplished: achieved or completed

enthusiasm: passion or fascination

"Yeah, but it hasn't really kicked in yet," Nate replied. Kristen couldn't help noticing that he kept glancing at her in the mirror, but she couldn't tell if it was out of curiosity or **irritation**. "Can you move to the right?" he asked. He was only trying to see out the back window.

"Oh. Sure," Kristen said, sitting back in her seat and leaning toward the window.

"Thanks," Nate said. Then he turned to Macy. "Ready to go?"

"Whenever you are," Macy answered, and Nate immediately began to back out. When he shifted into first, his wheels started to spin on the snow and ice, but he took care of it quickly by letting up on the gas for a moment, allowing the car to roll forward slightly, and then applying the gas again, gently. At seventeen—or *maybe eighteen*, Kristen realized—he already seemed to be a fairly experienced driver.

Nate joined the **queue** of cars waiting to pull out of the student parking lot, and, while at a standstill, selected a CD and pressed it into the player that was mounted under the dash. After a few seconds, a familiar drumbeat echoed through the car, and Kristen recognized the song as an old Violent Femmes tune she'd always liked. She was just about to ask Nate which album he'd put in when she **glimpsed** Tracy, Luke, and Trevor up ahead. Tracy was sitting on the trunk of her car, Luke was standing in front of her, facing her with his arms on her waist, and Trevor was leaning against his Jeep, which was parked in the **adjacent** space. Traffic was moving slowly, and Kristen knew that if she didn't do something fast, they were going to spot her in the back of Nate Jacobs' car.

"Are you missing a CD case?" she asked hastily.

"No," Nate said.

"Oh, well . . . I think I see one under the seat. Here—I'll get it for you." With that, she dove forward, doubling over and pretending to fumble around under the passenger side seat for something.

---

irritation: annoyance
queue: line

glimpsed: partially saw
adjacent: nearby

When she turned her head, she could see Tracy out the driver side window—they were nearly up to her now. *Just another minute,* Kristen thought. "I can almost reach it," she said, keeping up the **façade** for Nate and Macy. Suddenly, the music stopped, and she heard the engine cut out.

"Get up," Nate said.

"Nate, what are you doing?" Macy asked.

"Get up, Kristen," Nate repeated.

Kristen glanced out the side window, aware that Nate had stopped the car right next to Tracy, Luke, and Trevor. "But I've almost got the CD case," she protested.

"I'm not missing a CD case," Nate said flatly, "and this is not a limo service for stuck-up princesses. Either sit up like a big girl or find another ride."

Kristen gazed out the window again, aware that Tracy was now staring at Nate's car, trying to figure out why he'd stopped. "Nate, I—"

"I'm not moving until you get up," he replied.

The cars behind them started to honk, and to Kristen's horror, Tracy was now pointing at Nate's car. More **precisely**, she was pointing at the backseat of Nate's car, at Kristen, and howling with laughter.

Kristen felt her cheeks, her face—her whole body—blush bright red and wished she could disappear, but it seemed that the only **option** she had was to sit up, which, slowly, she did. By this time, Macy had noticed Tracy's laughter and Kristen's shame and put the whole scene together.

"That girl is such a witch," she said. "I don't know why you care so much about what she thinks of you."

"Are you kidding?" Kristen asked. "How about because everyone in the school follows her lead," she **retorted**.

---

façade: appearance **option:** choice
precisely: exactly **retorted:** replied

"Not everyone," Macy said. "Come on, Nate. Let's get out of here."

"Gladly," Nate said. He turned the key in the ignition, bringing both the engine and the radio roaring back to life, and pulled out of the lot, leaving Tracy, her sidekicks and all the honking cars behind.

For a while, they drove in silence—aside from the loud bass and screeching vocals **emanating** from the radio—and Kristen sat in the back, feeling guilty for having tried to hide on the floor. Were they going to join the list of people giving her the permanent silent treatment now?

But after a few minutes, Macy finally spoke up. "I really need to pee," she said, crossing her legs and leaning forward.

"Why didn't you go back at the school?" Kristen asked. "The bathroom is right next to the main entrance. It only would have taken a second."

"I know," Macy said, "but I can't. I have to hold it."

Perplexed, Kristen glanced to the rearview mirror for Nate's reaction and caught him gazing right back at her. Their eyes met for a brief second before they both blinked away.

"I had to drink a bunch of water over the last hour to get ready for my sonogram, and I'm not supposed to pee until it's done."

"Oh my God," Kristen said. "How much longer do you have to wait? When are you having the sono . . . thingy?"

Macy giggled, which made Kristen feel a little better. Maybe she wasn't too **perturbed** by Kristen's **tactless** behavior after all. "Sonogram," she said, "and I don't have to wait long at all. We're here."

We are? Kristen thought. She followed the trajectory from Macy's pointing finger to the large brick **edifice** in front of them—Brooksfield Memorial Hospital. "What? I thought—," Kristen started. "Weren't we going to hang out or something?"

---

emanating: emitting
perplexed: puzzled

perturbed: upset
tactless: insensitive

edifice: building

"Or something," Macy answered as Nate swung his car into a space right in front of the building. "You have such good parking **karma**, Nate," she added, stepping onto the sidewalk.

Kristen hesitated for a moment, not sure if she was supposed to get out of the car or not. She'd thought they were going for coffee or something—not a doctor's appointment. Why on earth had Macy invited her along?

"You coming?" Nate asked, poking his head back in before shutting his door.

"Um, yeah, I guess," Kristen said, still feeling a little awkward about the fact that she'd been invited by a pregnant girl she barely knew to hang out at the hospital with her and her full bladder. It didn't exactly seem like a **customary** getting-to-know-you activity. And wait a second—why was Nate coming along? Was he just a friend who gave Macy rides to her appointments, or was he something more? Like, for instance, the baby's father?

Kristen swallowed, that last thought bothering her more than it should have. What did she care if Nate and Macy were a thing? Except she kind of felt bad for any baby having a guy like him for a father. He seemed so *angry* all the time.

What was it Dr. Griffin said about my anger issues? If there were a contest, Nate would beat her before they were even out of the gate.

All the way up to the hospital doors, through the hall, up in the elevator, and down to the ultrasound room, Kristen found herself **lagging** behind Nate and Macy, watching them for any sign of intimacy that went beyond that of simple friendship. They didn't seem to be walking all that close together, they weren't holding hands or linking arms, and they didn't exchange any **clandestine** smiles or secret looks as far as Kristen could tell. So what was the deal?

"Macy," an older woman with curly white hair, a chubby face, and a pink flowered lab coat called as they arrived. "It's so good to see you. How have you been since your last visit?"

---

karma: destiny
customary: usual

lagging: lingering

clandestine: secret

"Fine," Macy said, grinning. "I'm starting to get big, but I still feel great. Except that I have to pee." She glanced into the room the **technician** had just come out of. It appeared to be empty. "Is there a wait?" she asked.

"Not at all," the technician replied. "Come right in and we'll take care of you. Then you can go empty your bladder."

"Great. Thanks," Macy said. She turned to Nate. "Just give me a chance to get settled and ask a few questions," she said, and he nodded.

And then what? Kristen wondered. What was Nate supposed to do once Macy was settled? She watched as Macy followed the technician into the examination room, the door shutting behind them, and then she panicked as she realized that she was stuck in the otherwise empty waiting area with Nate.

If Nate felt weird about being alone with her, it wasn't **evident**. He just picked up a copy of *Sports Illustrated* that had to be at least eight weeks old—the standard doctor's office issue—and sat down in one of the green chairs to read. Following his lead, Kristen thumbed through a few of the magazines on the large square coffee table, but found little that **appealed** to her. Finally, she snagged a copy of *Highlights for Children* and sat down one chair away from Nate, setting herself to the task of finding the ten items hidden in the picture on the back cover.

The first three were easy, the second three a little more challenging, and the next three downright hard. The tenth item, however—a small triangular flag—was **virtually** impossible. Kristen sat staring at the picture, all five fingers extended on her left hand and four on her right, until the lines started to blur.

"Which one don't you have?" Nate asked.

"Hmm?" Kristen asked, glancing up at him. Again she was struck by how dark his brown eyes were—the irises barely **distinguishable** from the pupils.

---

technician: skilled person   **appealed:** pleased   **distinguishable:** discernible
evident: obvious   **virtually:** essentially

Nate darted a look at her nine fingers and then at the picture. "Which one do you need?"

"Oh—the little flag," Kristen said, stabbing her index finger at it. "But it's impossible to find. I've been looking for—"

"Got it," Nate said with a little nod. Then he went back to his *Sports Illustrated*.

Kristen stared at him, then down at the picture, then back again. "No way!" she said.

Nate paused in his reading and looked up. "Want me to show you?" he offered.

"No," Kristen said. Nate went back to his magazine, and she went back to the picture, **scanning** every inch of it for the flag, to no **avail**. "Okay. Show me," she finally said. Nate chuckled. He set his magazine on his lap and leaned toward Kristen.

"Right there," he said, his forearm grazing hers as he pointed. Kristen had to work to ignore the tingling **sensation** that shot up her arm when he came in contact with her, and she tried to distract herself by focusing on the part of the picture he was pointing to.

"That's not—," she started, but then she saw it. "Oh." There, hidden in the stripes of a zebra, was the triangular flag, pole and all. Kristen scowled.

"You asked," Nate told her.

"I know," Kristen said, but she couldn't help feeling a little **frustrated** that he had found it so easily when she'd been searching so long. Not to mention the fact that when sparks had shot up her arm where he'd **grazed** it, he hadn't seemed to notice a thing.

"Nate? Kristen?" the technician **beckoned**, opening the door. "Macy would like you to join her now."

Nate didn't hesitate at all. He stood up and started for the door right away, but Kristen was still uncertain as to why she was here in the first place. When Nate reached the door to the room where Macy was, he stopped and turned to Kristen.

---

scanning: examining   **sensation:** feeling   **grazed:** lightly touched
avail: profit or benefit   **frustrated:** discouraged   **beckoned:** called

"Come on," he said. Kristen squinted at him **tentatively**. "What are you waiting for? The girl needs to pee."

The technician chuckled, and Macy giggled, then groaned from inside the room. "Don't make me laugh, Nate," she admonished him. "I'm having a hard enough time as it is."

"Sorry," Nate apologized. "I was just trying to get Kristen in here."

"Kristen!" Macy called. "Get in here right now, and don't even think about **defying** a pregnant girl with a maxed-out bladder."

Not wanting to **rile** Macy any further, Kristen decided to **comply**. Slowly, she walked over to the door of the room where Macy was lying on a hospital bed and stepped inside. Nate was already on one side of the bed, so Kristen started to head for the other, but the technician stopped her.

"You'll have a better view if you stand next to Nate over there," she suggested. Kristen swallowed hard and tried to appear unfazed by the recommendation.

"Oh. Okay," she said, shuffling over next to Nate, careful not to get too close for fear of causing a shock to her system.

"Ready, Macy?" the technician asked.

"Mm-hmm. Show them," Macy said, her eyes positively glowing.

The technician took a small device that looked something like a computer mouse, except that it was slightly larger and rounder, and spread **conductive** petroleum jelly across its bottom. "We warmed this up today," she said, smiling at Macy.

"I noticed," Macy said. "Thanks."

Kristen watched as the older woman, whose nametag said Rosemary, placed the small paddle on Macy's **protruding** belly and began moving it slowly from side to side.

"I'm pretty big, huh?" Macy said. It took Kristen a minute to realize that she was the one being addressed—doubtless because she

---

tentatively: hesitantly   **rile:** upset   **conductive:** transmitting
defying: disobeying   **comply:** obey   **protruding:** bulging

was the only one in the room staring at Macy's **abdomen** as though an alien might **erupt** from it at any time.

"Yeah," she said with a nod. Macy wore such baggy clothes at school that it was impossible to **ascertain** the outline of her stomach. Kristen never would have guessed that it was so . . . *rotund*.

"Well, try to tear your eyes away for a second and check out the monitor." Macy was smiling at her, but Kristen felt like an **imbecile** for **gawking**.

"Sorry," she started, "I didn't mean to—*whoa*." The image on the monitor made Kristen forget what she was about to say. "Is that—?" She gaped at the x-ray picture of the **flailing** baby on the screen behind the technician, then gazed at Macy's belly and back again.

"It sure is," Rosemary answered. "**Energetic** little fellow today— look at those arms and legs go."

Kristen brought her hands to her face and continued to stare. It was difficult to imagine that the little being on the screen was **enclosed** in Macy's stomach, even though she knew that was the case. Still, it just seemed so **extraordinary**.

"This is the head," Rosemary said, pointing to the screen, "and here's the backbone—see all the little vertebrae? Here we have the right arm, the left arm, both legs and feet. Look, you can count the fingers and toes—five on every limb. And here, in the chest **cavity**, this little fluttery thing is the heart."

Kristen gasped. For a moment, she could actually see everything Rosemary was pointing out. Then the **fetus** shifted, or Macy or the technician shifted, and the image on the screen turned into what looked more like a photograph of a black hole.

"Now, if I get this just right," Rosemary said, repositioning the scanner on Macy's belly, "we should be able to hear the heartbeat." Kristen's eyes widened. "Here we go," Rosemary said.

Kristen watched the monitor, where a long, straight line had appeared. Suddenly, it began to **fluctuate** wildly, and the room was

---

abdomen: stomach and reproductive area
erupt: explode
ascertain: determine
rotund: rounded

imbecile: fool
gawking: staring
flailing: flapping
energetic: lively
enclosed: confined

extraordinary: amazing
cavity: opening
fetus: unborn baby
fluctuate: shift

filled with a quick and steady beat that sounded like someone rapidly turning a vacuum cleaner on and off underwater. "Oh my God," Kristen breathed, covering her gaping mouth with one hand. "It sounds like the ocean—like waves breaking on fast-forward. You should name the baby after the water. Maybe Ocean for a boy—Oceana if it's a girl." The words spilled out before she'd thought about what she was saying, but as soon as she stopped, she knew she'd said something wrong from the torn expression on Macy's face and the weird tension that suddenly filled the room.

"I'm not keeping it," Macy said, her voice a quiet rasp. "I'm giving the baby up for adoption."

Kristen felt her shoulders slump. "I'm so—"

"You couldn't have known," Macy interrupted.

Kristen knew she was right, but that didn't help the fact that Nate was staring at her like she was a complete **buffoon**.

* * * * *

Kristen slouched in the backseat of the car on the way home, but this time it wasn't because she was worried about being seen with Macy and Nate. She just felt like a complete jerk for blurting out baby names as if Macy were some regular, happily settled pregnant woman **ecstatically** experiencing a **deliberate** and much-desired pregnancy instead of the knocked-up sixteen-year-old that she was. *So stupid,* Kristen told herself over and over, unable to **comprehend** how she could have made such a **gaffe**.

She stared out the window at the **immense** pine trees lining the highway and listened to the hum of the wheels on the pavement. Nate hadn't even bothered with music this time around. It seemed the mood was too **somber** even for **angst**-ridden punk rock.

"At first I wanted to keep it," Macy said, shattering the silence. "Actually, that's not true. At first I just wanted it out of me."

---

buffoon: clown or fool   comprehend: understand   somber: serious
ecstatically: delightfully   gaffe: blunder   angst: anxiety
deliberate: planned   immense: enormous

Kristen sat up straight. "Oh, Macy, you don't have to explain," she said.

"I want to," Macy said. Her voice was slow and quiet.

Kristen sat still and waited. She had a feeling that at the rate she was going, the best move would be to speak as little as possible.

"When I first found out I was pregnant, I couldn't believe it. I kept looking in the mirror and thinking that the test had to be wrong, but I did three more and they all came out positive too, so I was pretty sure it wasn't a mistake."

Nate put on his right turn signal and took the exit for Derry—a town name that now made Kristen cringe because of the rumors going around school. Macy was quiet while he slowed to a stop and waited for a green light so that he could turn left on Route 1, but once the car was moving again, she continued her story.

"I didn't know what to do or who to tell. It felt like I was in a movie or something, you know? Like none of it was actually real, like I was watching someone else go through the whole thing, and there were times, in school or at home when I was watching TV or something, when I'd actually forget about it for a second. But then I'd remember and I'd feel so . . . *trapped*, so hopeless. A couple of times I hit my stomach as hard as I could. And a part of me even hoped, as crazy as it sounds, that I would go to the doctor for a professional test and someone would say, 'Pregnant? Oh, no. The reason your tests are coming up positive is because you have a tumor on your ovary.' It seemed like hearing that would be such a relief— so much easier to deal with than being sixteen and pregnant. No one blames cancer on you, you know? But if you're pregnant everyone figures you did something to deserve it."

Kristen listened **intently**, one part **riveted**, one part feeling like she was being given information to which she shouldn't have **access**. One thing seemed increasingly certain—this baby wasn't

---

intently: seriously   **riveted:** fascinated   **access:** admission

Nate's. It just didn't seem like Macy would say all of this right in front of him like that, if it was.

"Finally, I told my friend Ellen," Macy continued, "and she was really sympathetic and everything, but then other people started coming up to me and asking me if it was true, so I knew she'd been talking about it behind my back. She tried to deny it, but I hadn't told anyone else, so I knew she was the one spreading rumors about me." She turned her head toward Kristen. "Unfortunately, the ones about me were true."

Kristen remembered when she'd first heard that Macy was pregnant about two months ago—she'd actually laughed. In fact, Kristen realized, she might even have made a comment like, "Hasn't she heard of a condom?" or something to that effect. "I'm sorry," she said lamely.

"Yeah, it kind of sucked," Macy said, "but at least it made me realize that I needed to figure out what I was going to do. In a way, all the gossip made it more real to me. All the people whispering in the halls made me realize that I needed to deal with it because it wasn't going to go away on its own. So . . . I went home and told my aunt."

"What'd she say?" Kristen asked, **circumspectly**.

"She told me I was stupid and that I'd never been anything but trouble, but even so, she said she wasn't going to let me ruin my life. As far as Aunt Frida was concerned, abortion was the only option, and at first I thought she was right. I was tired of thinking about it and I was sick of being pointed at. I just wanted the whole thing to be over with. So we got in the car and headed for Planned Parenthood, and when we got in there, Frida marched right up to the desk and told the woman standing there that I had come for an abortion.

"The receptionist took one look at me and I burst out crying, so she guided me into a back room and asked Aunt Frida to stay in the waiting room. Then she sent in a nurse who talked to me for a while

circumspectly: cautiously

and explained that they didn't just do abortions upon request and that I'd have to go through a whole examination and counseling process first. She kept asking me if I understood what she was saying, and I just kept nodding. I didn't even feel like I was really there—it was weird.

"So anyway, about forty-five minutes later, she brought me back out to Aunt Frida and explained that I'd need to come back a few more times before they could schedule any kind of procedure, and Frida was furious. She kept asking them why they couldn't just take care of it—she was my legal guardian and she was ready to sign whatever release forms they needed right then and there. But the nurse who'd talked with me just kept telling her that we'd have to come back, and somehow, she finally convinced my aunt to take me home.

"Frida was horrible to me from that point forward, because she was convinced that I had said something to keep them from giving me the abortion. She told me that I'd better not cry the next time we went in or I was going to ruin everything. Meanwhile, everyone was talking about me in school, pointing and laughing every time I walked by, and when I got home in the afternoon, Frida would start in, telling me I deserved everything people were saying about me and that I'd brought it all on myself."

"Oh my God," Kristen said, shaking her head. "I can't even imagine."

"Yeah, it was pretty bad. But then the next time I went into Planned Parenthood, after they did an exam and told me I was about eight weeks along, a counselor came in and started discussing options with me. She told me all about abortion—what the process was like, what kind of instruments they used, what kind of **anesthesia** I'd need, possible **complications**, everything. But she didn't stop there. She also talked to me about teens who decide to keep

---

anesthesia: painkiller   **complications:** problems

their babies, and finally, she told me about Our Choice. As soon as I heard about it, I knew that was what I wanted to do."

"So, you said Our Choice is a shelter for pregnant teens, right?" Kristen asked.

"Right," Macy agreed. "It's a shelter for teens who've decided to let their pregnancies go full term but don't have anywhere to live. And Aunt Frida had been pretty clear about the fact that if I wanted to stay in her house, I needed to get an abortion ASAP, and I just didn't feel like that was something I could do. I mean, I understand it's a choice that some people make, and I wouldn't judge anyone who decided that's what they needed to do—especially now that I know how difficult it is to be in that position. But somehow I just knew it wasn't the right choice for me. So I told Aunt Frida what I wanted to do. She gave me an **ultimatum**—end the pregnancy or find a new place to live—and I chose the second option. That was about three months ago, and I've been living at Our Choice ever since."

When Macy had finished speaking, Kristen couldn't help feeling that the heaviness of her words still hung in the **cramped** space of Nate's car. She cracked her window despite the light snow that was now falling and let the cold air wash over her face.

"Wow," she said finally, rolling her window back up. "So, is the shelter . . . nice?" she asked, for lack of a better word.

Macy nodded. "Yeah, it's okay. It's an old Victorian house that the director **renovated**. There are eight bedrooms on the second and third floors, and most of us have roommates. I think there are thirteen of us living there right now—not all from New Hampshire, though. A couple of the girls are from Massachusetts, and there's even one from New York."

"Wow," Kristen said again. All other words seemed to have **vanished** from her vocabulary.

---

ultimatum: stipulation or condition

cramped: confined or tight
renovated: restored

vanished: disappeared

"And there's an adoption agency right next door that works in **conjunction** with the shelter," Macy continued, "so that anyone who wants to go that route has access to all the services they offer. I'm doing an open adoption, and the couple that's taking my—I mean *the*—baby seems really nice. They're from Vermont and they live in a huge farmhouse with something like fourteen acres of land. It's gorgeous—they've shown me pictures. They already have a nursery decorated and everything. They're going to be able to give this baby such a good home—so much better than anything I could offer. And I still get to be involved to some **extent**. They're going to keep me updated and even let me visit, and they plan to let the baby know I'm its **biological** mom, even though they're going to be its parents."

Macy actually smiled as she talked about the whole situation, and it seemed like she had managed to work everything out. But there was one thing that still invited **conjecture**. "What about the father?" she blurted out.

The smile on Macy's face vanished, and Kristen realized she'd messed up the whole keeping-her-mouth-shut plan. "He's not involved," Macy said after a moment. "I told him I was pregnant, but he said there was no way it was his, so I just left it at that."

"I'm sorry, Macy—it's none of my business," Kristen said.

Macy shook her head. "It's a fair question," she said. "It's just not my favorite topic."

Kristen pressed her eyes closed, feeling like an idiot yet again and wishing that she could manage to think before she spoke. When she opened them again, she caught Nate scowling at her in the rearview mirror and realized he was probably thinking the same thing. And somehow, knowing that he too thought she was a **dolt** made her feel about five hundred times worse.

---

conjunction: connection   **biological:** genetic   **dolt:** fool
extent: degree   **conjecture:** guesses

"Did you get home before your mom called yesterday?" Macy asked, setting her tray on the lunch table next to Kristen's the next day.

"Uh, yeah," Kristen stammered, gazing up at Macy, completely dumbfounded. She'd assumed that after all of her **faux pas** yesterday afternoon, Macy wouldn't be begging her to hang out again anytime soon. Especially since there had been virtually no conversation—except Kristen telling Nate when to turn left or right in order to get to her mom's apartment—once Kristen had asked about the baby's **paternity**.

Macy started to pull out a chair, then hesitated. "Is it okay if I sit here?" she asked, catching Kristen's **bewildered** stare.

"Oh—yeah, of course," Kristen said, shaking the dazed look off her face. "I just thought, you know, I was so nosy and everything, I kind of figured—"

"Don't worry about it," Macy said, sitting down. "You weren't being nosy. I was telling you everything because I wanted to. I've never really talked about it with anyone other than counselors and the other girls at the shelter. I guess I just wanted to tell someone a little more . . . *normal*."

Kristen laughed. "So you chose the school slut?"

"You're not the school slut any more than I am," Macy said. "Although it probably *was* because of all the rumors that I felt comfortable talking to you. It just seemed like you'd understand, and like you wouldn't judge me, you know? It's the same with Nate. He gets judged all the time, so he's really good about keeping an open mind."

---

faux pas: blunder   **paternity:** fatherhood   **bewildered:** puzzled

"Yeah, I guess," Kristen said, even though she couldn't help feeling like Nate had already made up his mind about her, and she was fairly certain his opinion wasn't a **favorable** one. Every time he looked at her, it seemed like he was rolling his eyes.

"So what are you doing today after school?" Macy asked.

Kristen drew back slightly. "I'm not sure," she started. She wasn't sure if she was up for another doctor's visit.

Macy smiled. "Don't worry—it's nothing intense this time. I just need to get some clothes. The shelter gave me some money so that I could go to a secondhand shop and pick up a few things. I'm getting a little big for these," she said, stretching out the waistband of her sweatpants, "and supposedly the Goodwill on Mayhew Street has a lot of **maternity** stuff."

"Oh, okay." It was hard to believe that her social options had been reduced to viewing sonograms and shopping for maternity clothes. It was even harder to believe that she was considering saying yes. "I'm still grounded, but—"

"Hey," Nate said to Macy as he sat down next to her. He gave Kristen a nod—barely a nod, really, but at least it wasn't **hostile**. Apparently, as stupid as he thought she was, he wasn't holding it against her. "You still need a ride tonight?"

"If you can give me one," Macy said. Kristen swirled her spoon around in her yogurt, trying to tell herself that she had been ready to say yes even before she'd heard that Nate might be coming along, but she wasn't entirely convinced that was the case.

"I can, but it'll have to wait until three-thirty. Miller wants me to stay after and help one of the janitors power-spray the side of the building."

"Where you redecorated?" Macy asked with a smirk.

"Yeah." Nate nodded, showing no sign whatsoever that he found the situation amusing.

---

favorable: good   **maternity:** motherhood   **hostile:** unfriendly

"Okay," Macy said. "That works for me—does it work for you, Kristen?"

"Sure," Kristen answered, even though she knew she'd be cutting it close if they didn't even leave the school until three-thirty. Yesterday her mother had called at four-thirty on the dot.

"Okay, cool," Nate said. "I'll see you then."

Kristen watched him walk out of the cafeteria, his black hair scruffy around the collar of his black leather jacket.

"He's a piece of work," Macy said. "Dresses like the Angel of Death, but he's actually a pretty sweet guy."

Kristen nodded. He did seem pretty sweet—to Macy, at least. But somehow, Kristen didn't think she stood much of a chance of ever seeing his soft side. And for some strange reason, she found that thought **extremely** disappointing.

*   *   *   *   *

"What'd you get?" Nate asked when Kristen and Macy crawled into the car after their shopping **excursion**.

"Check it out," Macy said, opening one of the recycled plastic bags the people at Goodwill had packed her clothing into. "Brown maternity overalls, practically new," she said, **extracting** a huge bundle of wide-wale corduroy fabric from one of the bags. "A wool jumper, a new shirt," she continued, "and—these are the best of all, Kristen found them—maternity *jeans!*"

Macy held up a pair of faded blue jeans that looked completely normal except for the fact that there was a section of light blue stretch fabric where the zipper and button would normally have been. "The pregnancy panel is kind of weird," Macy admitted, "but as long as I wear long shirts, it won't show."

Nate nodded in **approbation**. "Whatever makes you happy," he said.

---

extremely: intensely   **extracting:** withdrawing   **approbation:** approval
excursion: trip

"It was awesome," Macy said. "It usually takes me forever to find something that I like, and even then I have no idea what I could wear it with, but Kristen just sailed through there grabbing stuff off the racks and telling me what went together and what didn't. I'm going to bring you with me *every* time I shop," Macy gushed. "Maybe you should too, Nate," she suggested. "She might be able to find you something to wear that isn't black."

Nate narrowed his eyes. "I like black," he said. There was an awkward moment, and then he added, "It goes with everything, you know," a hint of **irony** in his voice.

Simultaneously, Macy and Kristen burst into laughter. The idea of Nate giving a moment's thought to **coordinating** his outfits was **hilarious**. "What—you think I don't care how I look?" Nate asked, still with an air of mock **sobriety**. "I'll have you know I **agonize** over my appearance each and every morning," he said, sending Macy and Kristen into a fresh round of giggles.

When their laughter had finally died down, Kristen realized that Nate was heading the wrong way to drop her off. "Oops—my mom's is back there," she told him, gesturing over her shoulder with her thumb. "But you can just turn around at that gas station."

"Actually, I was planning to drop Macy off first, if that's okay," Nate said.

Kristen's skin prickled, and suddenly she felt like her whole body was on **alert**. "Oh, uh, all right," she said as **offhandedly** as possible, even though all she could think about was being alone in the car with Nate for the approximately seven-minute drive between Macy's shelter and Kristen's mom's apartment. And she couldn't help wondering if Nate was thinking the same thing. Had he made a **calculated** decision to drop Macy off first so that he and Kristen would be alone?

When Macy got out, Kristen hesitated for a minute, wondering whether she should switch to the front seat or not. "I'll see you guys

---

irony: wit or sarcasm **sobriety:** seriousness **offhandedly:** casually
coordinating: synchronizing **agonize:** struggle **calculated:** deliberate
hilarious: exceedingly funny **alert:** watch

tomorrow," Macy called. "Thanks!" Then she bounded up the walk, swinging her **parcels** back and forth.

"Should I . . . sit up there?" Kristen asked, pointing to the seat Macy had just vacated.

"If you want," Nate said with a shrug, and it really seemed like it didn't make a difference to him one way or another. "But whatever you're going to do, just do it," he said. "I have to stop at Hot Wax before they close. My headphones broke last night."

"Oh," Kristen said, her spirits sinking. Hot Wax was a music store just down the road from her mom's place. No wonder he'd wanted to drop Macy off first. It wouldn't have made sense for him to drive Kristen home, drive back through town to the shelter, and then head back out again to the music store. Suddenly, sitting in the front didn't seem like such a **monumental feat**.

She hopped out of the backseat, jumped into the front, and fastened her seat belt. "All set," she said, as Nate shifted into first and pulled a quick U-turn.

"So," Nate said at the first stoplight. "You and Macy are hanging out now."

"I guess," Kristen said.

"That's cool. She could use a good friend." Kristen glanced sideways at Nate. She wasn't sure that she and Macy **qualified** as friends yet, but at the same time, she found it hard to believe that they'd only known each other for two days.

"You seem like a pretty good friend," Kristen offered.

Nate cocked his head. "Yeah, but it's not the same."

"The same as what?"

"I don't know, it just seems like she could use a female friend, you know? Someone who understands more about being pregnant and stuff."

---

parcels: packages   **feat:** achievement   **qualified:** fit
monumental: outstanding

"Whoa—look, I know there are a lot of rumors going around about me," Kristen said, "but no matter what you've heard, I'm not pregnant."

Nate chuckled. "Nah, I haven't heard that one yet. But I could **initiate** a fresh round of stories for you tomorrow if you want."

"Thanks," Kristen said, "but I don't think my *friends* need any more **ammunition**."

"Some friends," Nate said.

"I thought they were," Kristen said. But then she **reflected** upon her relationships with Tracy, Stephanie, and Leah over the last three years. "Actually, you know what? I guess I really didn't."

Nate glanced over at her as he took a right turn onto her street. "What do you mean?"

"I don't know. Just that they used to be good friends, way back in middle school, you know? But I guess I haven't really felt close to any of them since then. Except maybe Leah, but even she . . ." Kristen let her voice trail off. For a moment, she'd forgotten Nate was there, and it had been more like she was thinking out loud than actually having a conversation with anyone. "Sorry," she said. "I don't mean to bore you with the **minutiae** of my life."

Nate pulled up to the curb in front of Ms. Graham's condo. "No problem," he said. "I've got time. But you don't," he added, pointing to the clock on his dash.

"Four forty-five! Oh, man, I'm in trouble," Kristen said, jumping out the car.

"Hey—what are you doing this weekend?" Nate asked. The question stopped Kristen dead.

She stared back at him, unable to form a response. Was he asking her out? Nate was kind of interesting, yeah, and she didn't mind thinking he wanted to be around her. But there was no way she could actually *date* someone like him. Then she remembered—it didn't matter. "Cleaning my father's garage. I'm still grounded."

---

initiate: start

ammunition: advantageous points for an argument

reflected: meditated

minutiae: minor details

"Oh, right," Nate said. "Too bad. I thought maybe we could get together—you know, all three of us. It would be good for Macy. I think weekends at the shelter are pretty **dreary**."

Ah, the three of us, Kristen thought. That was a relief . . . right? But it made sense, anyway. Kristen and Nate barely knew each other. And they had nothing in common. "Yeah, I bet they are," Kristen agreed. "Well, maybe next weekend."

"Yeah. Maybe," Nate said. He held her gaze for what seemed longer than necessary, and finally Kristen had to look away.

"Thanks for the ride," she said.

"Anytime," he said.

Kristen pushed the car door shut, gave a brief wave, and headed up the walkway. When she heard Nate's Volvo pull away, she had to fight the urge to turn around and watch him go. *What's wrong with me?* she found herself wondering as she unlocked the town house door. Was she actually attracted to this guy? And if so, why?

She barely knew him, but he was nothing like the J. Crew guys she'd dated in the past. He dressed all in black, listened to angry punk rock, took vocational classes, and belonged to a group for at-risk youth. Granted, Kristen was in the group too, but that wasn't the point.

"I can't believe you actually thought he was going to ask you out," Kristen told herself. "Get a grip, Carmichael."

Being attracted to someone so completely different was **futile**, and if she was developing some kind of a crush on Nate, she'd better get over it. Especially since he didn't seem to feel the same way.

---

dreary: dismal   **futile:** useless

"How'd the cleaning go?" Nate asked when Kristen walked into Dr. Griffin's room the following Tuesday.

"Huh?" Kristen said, drawing a blank. Then it hit her. "Oh—my dad's garage," she said. She hadn't seen Nate since he'd dropped her off last Thursday, and she'd almost forgotten that she'd told him about her big weekend plans. "It went pretty well, actually. It only took me a day and half."

"Cool," Nate said. "So, you still on track for getting ungrounded this weekend?"

Kristen blinked. He was getting straight to the point. And what was he doing here early? It had seemed like his style was showing up to the group late. Had he shown up when he did in order to ask her about next weekend before anyone else got there?

Before she could reply, Macy walked in, and Kristen remembered that Nate had been really hung up on Kristen being a friend to her. "Yeah. Actually, I think I'm more or less ungrounded right now," she said. "My mom sent me out to pick up a pizza last night, and she even let me stop at the bookstore to get a magazine."

"That's awesome, Kristen," Macy said. She sat down in the orange chair next to Nate. "Pull up a beanbag," she said, pointing to the space on the opposite side of her chair from Nate.

Kristen had been eyeing the vacant space on Nate's other side and trying to **determine** how she could **maneuver** herself into it without the move appearing **contrived**, but she decided Macy's suggestion was probably a better one. She had, after all, come to the conclusion three separate times over the course of the weekend that being interested in Nate was a bad idea.

---

determine: decide

maneuver: navigate or guide

contrived: planned

Desultorily, she grasped a loose fold of the red beanbag she'd used last week and tossed it down next to Macy's chair. Just in time too, because as soon as she was seated—she managed it a little more gracefully this week—Dr. Griffin walked in, followed shortly by the other members of the group.

"Anyone have any news?" he asked.

Somewhat **timidly**, but with more **composure** than Kristen had witnessed last week, Macy raised her hand. "Yes, Macy?"

"Over the weekend I went to this childbirth education class, and they showed a film of a woman giving birth." Everyone, including Dr. Griffin, watched Macy **expectantly**.

"And . . . was it good?" Dr. Griffin asked.

"Was there nudity?" Mikey asked. "'Cause if there's nudity, you should call me up the next time they're showing one of those."

"You're such a perv, Mikey," Lindsey said, twisting the stud in her nose.

"All right," Dr. Griffin said, holding out both hands. "Was there something about the movie you wanted to discuss, Macy?"

Kristen looked up at Macy, whose typically bright blue eyes looked **dull** today, and noticed for the first time that she was visibly **distraught**. "Are you okay, Macy?" she asked.

Macy inhaled a **shuddering** breath, her bottom lip **quivering**, and on the **exhale** she began to cry. Kristen felt like she should do something—put her arm around Macy, hold her hand, touch her leg, *something*, but she wasn't **quite** sure what.

"Do you want to talk about it, Macy?" Dr. Griffin asked. Macy had buried her face in her hands, but her nod was still **perceptible**. Alice grabbed the tissues from the end table beside her and passed them around the circle. Kristen watched, surprised at how quietly everyone was moving and how concerned they all looked. Even Mikey, who seemed to have a wise comment for everything, was watching Macy with **consternation**.

---

desultorily: sluggishly
timidly: nervously
composure: calmness
expectantly: anxiously
dull: listless

distraught: upset
shuddering: trembling or convulsive
quivering: trembling or shaking

exhale: breathe out
quite: completely
perceptible: detectable
consternation: dismay or anxiety

Macy procured a tissue from the box when it arrived at her chair and blew her nose a couple of times. Then, with tears still clouding her eyes, she looked up at the group. "I feel so stupid," she said.

Kristen glanced at Mikey and Lindsey, but neither one of them took the **opportunity** to tell Macy that she looked stupid too. Instead, to Kristen's surprise, they were both watching Macy silently with what appeared to be genuine warmth. Then again, it wasn't all that shocking. Who could be mean to a crying pregnant girl, anyway? *Aside from the jerks I used to hang around with,* Kristen thought.

"Like I said," Macy went on, her voice quaking, "we watched this video, and . . . this is going to sound so stupid," she said, "but all of a sudden it **occurred** to me—I'm going to have a baby." Macy started crying all over again, snatching tissue after tissue from the box while everyone in the room stared at her with **perplexed** expressions.

"I'm confused, Macy," Dr. Griffin said when she'd finally calmed down again. "What do mean when you say that it suddenly occurred to you that you're going to have a baby? Do you mean that up until now it hasn't seemed real, or . . . something else?"

Macy shook her head. "No, it's not that," she said, dabbing at her nose with a crumpled-up tissue ball. "It's been real to me for a while now," she said, patting her stomach and giving a weak laugh. Others in the room followed suit, relieved to have a chance to **vent** a little of the **tension**.

"Then what is it?" Dr. Griffin asked.

"It's that—oh, God," Macy said, taking another quivering breath. "I'm going to have to *have* it," she said finally. "I have to actually *give birth*, and I'm not sure I can do it. You should have heard this woman in the video. She was screaming and groaning—she was in so much pain. I just don't see how I'm going to—" Her voice broke off and the tears took over again.

---

opportunity: moment or time   **perplexed:** puzzled   **tension:** nervousness
occurred: struck   **vent:** relieve

This time, while Kristen was sitting there feeling like she should do something, Lindsey got up from her beanbag on the **opposite** side of the room and walked straight over to Macy. Gently, she touched Macy's elbow and nudged her over a little so that she could perch on the edge of her seat. Then she put her arm around Macy's shoulder and gave her a big hug.

"Of course you can do it," Lindsey said. "It's the most natural thing in the world. When my sister was pregnant, her doctor told her that women in China squat right down in the rice fields and have their kids. And then they go back to picking again like nothing ever happened."

"Well, I'm not sure that's exactly how *all* women give birth in China, but you do bring up a good point, Lindsey," Dr. Griffin said. "Not that anyone expects *you* to harvest rice during childbirth, Macy," he added. "Unless, of course, you find it relaxing."

Macy made a choked noise that sounded like something halfway between a sob and a laugh.

"I saw my sister being born," Ellen Stank said. "My mom had her at home with a midwife. It was kind of scary to watch, because my mom was moaning and stuff, but it couldn't have been too bad. She had three more kids after that."

"That's true," Alice piped up. "If it was really terrible, everyone would just have one child and never do it again, right?"

"Yeah, and besides, can't they give you a whole bunch of drugs?" Mikey asked. "You probably won't feel a thing."

Again, Macy sob-laughed, and after she blew her nose, Kristen was glad to see that she was actually smiling. "Thanks, you guys," she said, her voice **muted** from all the crying. "You're all right. People have babies every day. I guess I just feel kind of alone sometimes, you know?"

"It's a valid feeling," Dr. Griffin said, nodding. "Everyone feels alone from time to time, but it's important to remember that you

---

opposite: facing   muted: subdued

aren't." Lindsey, all blue-black hair and pierced flesh, smiled at Macy and gave her another squeeze.

"Thanks," Macy said.

"Well, Macy, it just so happens that you've provided a perfect introduction to one of the things I'd like to talk about today," Dr. Griffin said. "I'd like everyone to take a minute and think about what it's like to feel overwhelmed by something."

Kristen thought about the way it had felt to learn about all the rumors that were being spread about her. How **exposed** she felt walking down the hallway and knowing that everyone was laughing at her. How alone she felt practically everywhere she went, and how her parents were way too wrapped up in their own lives to even realize that anything was wrong.

"Okay," Dr. Griffin said. "Now I'd like you to try to think of something you could do to help yourself calm down when that feeling hits. It can be anything—anything that brings you peace or makes you feel grounded. It might be a specific person you would try to spend time with or an activity you would engage in. . . . When you've got something, raise your hand, and when everybody's ready, we'll go around and share our ideas."

Kristen didn't even have to think. Before Dr. Griffin had finished his first sentence, she'd already come up with surfing. But she didn't want to be the first to raise her hand, so she waited until three or four others were in the air before adding hers. After another minute, everyone had a hand in the air.

"Macy, why don't you start," Dr. Griffin said, "and we'll go this way." He **indicated** with his hand that Nate would be next, which meant Kristen, on Macy's other side, would be last. Lindsey had gone back to her seat once Macy had everything under control.

"I talk when I'm upset or overwhelmed," Macy said. "The only problem is that I'm not always comfortable talking to other girls at the shelter because they've got their own issues and they're not

---

exposed: unprotected   **indicated:** showed

always the best listeners. And the counselors aren't always available. But I do have you guys every Tuesday, and, as **trite** as it sounds, I'm really grateful for that."

"Thank you, Macy," Dr. Griffin said. Kristen noticed that everyone else in the group, with the exception of Lindsey and Nate, was looking down at their shoes. They obviously weren't **accustomed** to receiving compliments.

"Nate?" Dr. Griffin prompted.

"I paint," Nate said. Then he stared straight ahead. It seemed **apparent** that he didn't plan to **elaborate**, but Kristen wondered what kind of painting he did, aside from Elvises on the sides of school buildings, of course.

From Nate, Dr. Griffin moved on to Ellen, who, quiet as she was, claimed she liked to sing to relieve stress. Next was Alice, who said she always cleaned her room when stress hit, and then Lindsey, who apparently preferred to go running. Kristen had **presumed** that she went out and got a new piercing whenever she felt stressed.

At first, Mikey tried to claim he couldn't think of anything, but finally Dr. Griffin **wheedled** out of him that he liked to rap. Everyone seemed pretty entertained by the idea of Mikey hanging out alone rapping to himself, but Dr. Griffin managed to get them all calmed down again in time for Kristen to share before the bell rang.

"I surf," Kristen said plainly, intending to follow Nate's cue and avoid further explanation.

"You surf? What kind of sites?" Mikey asked, raising his eyebrows.

"Not the Internet," Kristen told him. "The ocean."

But instead of nodding or saying, *ohhh*, Mikey looked even more puzzled. "The ocean?" he echoed. "In New Hampshire?"

"Yeah," Kristen said. "There are lots of good spots."

"There are?" Lindsey asked. She was gazing at Kristen like she was crazy, just the way Kristen's ex-friends always had.

---

trite: hackneyed or unoriginal
accustomed: familiar with
apparent: clear

elaborate: go into details
presumed: supposed or assumed

wheedled: cajoled or persuaded

"Yes. There are," Kristen said.

"Huh. I thought surfing was a West Coast thing," Lindsey said. "I didn't know that anybody did it around here."

Kristen sighed. If she had a dollar for every time she'd heard someone make that **declaration**, she could quit school, retire, and spend the next sixty years surfing. "That's what everybody thinks," she said, "but East Coast surfing is just as good. It's just colder."

"And it must be a much shorter season too," Lindsey said.

"Actually, no," Kristen replied. "A lot of people winter surf around here. Well—not a lot, but there must be about twelve of us locally. And I know there are a bunch in Maine and Massachusetts too."

"You go into the ocean in the winter?" Lindsey said. "Are you nuts?"

"Hey, maybe you oughtta share some of the drugs you're on with Macy for when she goes into labor," Mikey suggested.

"Mikey," Dr. Griffin said, shaking his head.

"What? She's **insane**," Mikey said. "Why else would someone go surfing in New Hampshire in the winter?"

"Maybe Kristen can **enlighten** us," Dr. Griffin suggested. "Kristen," he began, "is there anything you could say to those of us who won't even dip our toes into the ocean in August to convince us that surfing in the winter could actually be enjoyable?"

Kristen looked around the room, amazed to see that everyone was actually leaning forward, **anticipating** her answer. Even Nate appeared interested in what she might have to say, and he was staring at her **intently**, a fact that made Kristen shiver.

"Well," Kristen started. She didn't usually like being the center of attention, but this time it was different. No one had ever asked her to talk about surfing before. "I'm not sure I can change anyone's mind about surfing—especially if you don't really like the ocean—

| **declaration:** assertion or announcement | **insane:** crazy **enlighten:** instruct | **anticipating:** awaiting **intently:** keenly |

but I can tell you why I do it. I surf because . . . it challenges me, I guess. Physically and mentally, you know?"

Kristen glanced around at the faces that were still watching her, **bemused**, and knew that she hadn't done a very good job of explaining what surfing was all about.

"It's like this," she said, squinting up at the ceiling and trying to find the right words. "The ocean is like this big, powerful thing that no one's ever really explored. We don't really know what's way down there in the depths, and we don't have any control over it. It's like, it's wild and **untamed**, you know? And when you're out there on a surfboard—just a little board, no engine, no motor, no steering wheel—it's just you and the ocean, and you have to come to terms with it. You have to respect its power and find your balance, and nobody else can do it for you. They can give you advice and tell you how to get started and stuff, but every time you go out, it's just you and the ocean."

Kristen shook her head and sighed, thinking that her explanation was growing **redundant**. "I don't know," she said. "I'm not doing a very good job of explaining it. I've never tried to put it into words before."

"But surfing is something that brings you peace?" Dr. Griffin asked.

"Definitely," Kristen said.

"And you do it all winter?" Ellen asked.

Kristen nodded. "Yeah. Like I said, there's a handful of us that do it year-round here. Most people go out in the mornings, around 5 A.M."

"Five A.M.!" Mikey exclaimed. "Do you do that?"

"Sometimes," Kristen said. "I like to try to surf before school when I'm at my dad's. He lives near Perkins Beach, and there's a really good spot there."

"Wow," Mikey said. "You're hard-core—I never would have guessed it."

---

bemused: puzzled   **untamed:** aggressive   **redundant:** unnecessary

Just then the bell rang, and everyone jumped out of their seats—everyone except Macy, whose stomach seemed to have gotten even bigger over the weekend. "Hey, Kristen," she said. "Since you're not really grounded anymore, do you want to go for coffee after school today? I'll be drinking herbal tea, but you can go for the espresso jolt if you want."

"I would," Kristen said, "but I'm staying at my dad's tonight, which means he's picking me up after school."

"Did you say you're staying at your dad's?" Nate asked, joining them after kicking his beanbag chair back to the wall.

"Mm-hmm," Kristen said.

"Yeah, so it looks like it's just you and me for coffee, Nate," Macy said.

Kristen felt a stab of disappointment. She would have liked to be able to hang out with Macy a little more. *And Nate as well.* Macy was becoming a friend, and there was something about Nate that made Kristen feel drawn to him. *And whatever it is, I've got to get over it,* Kristen told herself. Because as disappointed as she was to be missing an opportunity to hang out with him, Nate didn't appear **disconcerted** at all.

---

disconcerted: upset

Chapter Fourteen

It's just you and the ocean, Kristen thought as she paddled out the next morning at 5 A.M. Had she really said that out loud? More than once? *I'm such a dork,* she thought, working her arms **feverishly**.

She couldn't quite **comprehend** how Dr. Griffin had gotten her to share all that stuff about surfing with the group. She wasn't a sharer. She didn't even like the word. *Share.* The very sound of it was **infantilizing**.

The waves were kind of mushy this morning, with a stiff onshore wind making things even worse. But Kristen was determined to get out there and give it a try. It wasn't an ideal first day back, but when her father had told her last night that he and her mother had decided to lift the grounding early since she'd been **adhering** to it so **laudably** (they hadn't been **apprised** of her **jaunts** to the hospital and Goodwill with Macy and Nate), Kristen had set her alarm for four forty-five immediately. After a week and half of no surfing at all, nothing could have precluded her coming out.

She continued paddling out to the break, the cool wind whipping her face all the way. *I should have grabbed some of those hand warmers from Ken,* she thought, feeling the chill in her bones, even though she'd only been in the water for about fifteen minutes. Of course, before she could pick up hand warmers, she'd have to con one of her parents out of a few extra dollars—she'd only managed to save eight from last week's lunches.

Nearly at the break, Kristen stopped paddling and looked around. It was pretty soupy, but there seemed to be a pretty clean set on the way in. Plunging her arms back into the water, Kristen

---

feverishly: fervently or enthusiastically
comprehend: understand

infantilizing: treating one as immature
adhering: sticking

laudably: admirably
apprised: told
jaunts: trips

paddled with all of her might straight toward the incoming waves, moving out of the channel and into position.

Again, she'd managed to hit the beach at a time when no one else was around—probably because the conditions were less than **ideal**—so there was no need to line up or be concerned about anybody dropping in.

As the wave approached and Kristen felt her nose angling skyward, she popped up and took off down the face of the wave. It was only a two- or three-footer, not nearly as big as the ones she'd ridden last time, but it was big enough. Kristen executed a perfect bottom turn, which allowed her to build up her speed a little, and then carved her way across the face until it was too mushy to keep going.

Not bad, she thought, lying down on her board and paddling out to set up her next ride. She was almost to the break again, when something caught her eye on the shore. Glancing toward the small parking lot off to the side of the beach, Kristen could have sworn she saw an orange car. A bright orange car. A bright orange Volvo.

Get over yourself, Kristen, she thought. It was bad enough that she got all **flustered** whenever he was nearby; she certainly didn't need to start imagining that he was nearby when he wasn't. *You've got Nate Jacobs on the brain,* she told herself, *and you've got to get him off it.*

Striking at the water with her palms, she headed into another wave even smaller than the last. It didn't look like conditions were going to improve at all. If anything, they were getting worse. In all likelihood, this was the last surfable wave Kristen was going to get this morning, so she knew she had to make the best of it.

She popped up on the lip of the wave and rode it as long as she could before taking off down the face and cutting back into the pocket. From there, Kristen angled her board to the right, in the direction of the shore, intending to surf to the bottom, but the glimpse of orange she caught in her peripheral vision distracted her.

---

ideal: perfect

flustered: nervous or agitated

Stop it, she told herself, positive that she was turning what was probably just an orange traffic cone into Nate's Volvo in her mind. But as her board began to nosedive and she started to go down, she was almost certain that she saw not only an orange shape far too large to be a cone, but someone standing on the beach watching her. Someone dressed completely in black.

*　　*　　*　　*　　*

"That was pretty cool," Nate said as Kristen dragged her board out of the water.

She stared at him. "Thanks," she said. Then, without thinking, she added, "What are you doing here?"

Nate shrugged. "You seemed so, I don't know, *passionate* about surfing when you were talking about it in group, so I thought I'd come see what it was about." Kristen felt that strange fluttery feeling **wending** its way through her body again, and shivered **noticeably**. "You must be freezing," Nate said.

Kristen nodded. She was, but she was pretty sure that wasn't what had caused her to shudder.

"Grab your stuff and get in my car," he said. "I'll warm it up."

"Thanks, but"—Kristen shot a glance at her belongings—"I don't have any dry clothes. I usually just towel off, throw on my jacket and boots, and head back to my dad's to change."

"I've got clothes in my car," Nate offered.

"Are they all black?" Kristen asked.

Nate smirked. "Of course."

"I don't know," Kristen said. She glanced toward Nate's Volvo and tried to determine what time it was.

"It goes with everything," Nate reminded her, and Kristen laughed.

---

wending: traveling　　　　**noticeably:** visibly

"It's not the clothes that I'm worried about," she assured him. "It's just that I still need to get back to my dad's and shower and change and be ready to leave with him when he takes off at seven."

Nate extended his right arm and checked his watch. "It's six o'clock," he said. "You've got an hour."

Kristen calculated the minutes in her head: five to get back to her dad's, ten to shower, five to dress, five more to dry her hair, and ten to get all her stuff together and make some toast for the car ride. That gave her twenty-five minutes to spare. *Plenty of time to—*

"Come on," Nate said. "You can figure out what to do in the car. *I'm* going to freeze just looking at you if don't get dried off soon." He grabbed Kristen's surfboard and headed up the beach with it.

"Nate!" Kristen called, but he didn't look back. Quickly, she gathered up all of her things—boots, jacket, mittens, towel—and headed after him. By the time she got to his car, he had already propped her board against the side, gotten in, and turned on the heat full blast.

"Here," he said, handing her a pair of black, fully lined wind pants, a black T-shirt, and a black fleece sweatshirt. "You can change into these. I'll just . . . look over here." He gestured toward the ocean and turned his back to her so she could change.

As fast as possible, Kristen pulled off her booties, gloves, hood, and wet suit—no easy task with nearly numbed fingers and soaking wet skin—and changed into the clothes Nate had given her. "Done," she called as she hopped into the **blissfully** warm car. In a matter of seconds, Nate joined her, sliding into the driver's side seat.

"Here—you can take these too," he said, furnishing a pair of wool socks.

"Uh, Nate?" Kristen said, as she slid them on her feet. "I hate to break this to you, but these are gray."

---

blissfully: delightfully

"I prefer *light black*," he replied, completely **deadpan**. But in a moment, his **gorgeous** smile broke through. Kristen smiled back at him, **marveling** at his nutmeg eyes, his unruly black hair, and the day-old stubble on his chin. He really was attractive, not to mention funny, kind, and real. Why had Kristen allowed Tracy to convince her that people like Nate weren't worth her time? How many other cool people had she **disregarded** in the name of popularity? And most important, how much closer could Nate's mouth get before he was kissing her?

Not much, Kristen realized with a jolt as she felt the warmth of his skin. But instead of kissing her, he let his lips graze hers ever so lightly, trailing them along her cheek, her nose, her other cheek, and back toward her ear. When she felt the blast of his hot breath on her neck, the tingling sensation running through her body intensified.

"Nate," she whispered, but he placed two of his fingers on her lips.

"Shhh," he said, breathing into her ear. "I just want to kiss you." Kristen nodded and tried to answer him affirmatively, but all that came out was a raspy squeak. Even so, Nate seemed to understand.

Ever so gently, he kissed her neck just below her jawline, and then he planted a series of **dulcet** kisses along her closed eyelids. From there, **proceeding** down the bridge of her nose, he eventually reached her mouth, pressing his soft lips lightly into hers at first, and then, as Kristen parted her lips, more **resolutely**.

When he pulled away, Kristen was left leaning toward him, her eyes still closed, waiting patiently for another kiss.

"Six-thirty," Nate said, his voice low and soft.

Kristen kept her eyes closed and sat **immobilized**. "Hmm?"

---

deadpan: impassive
gorgeous: beautiful or exquisite
marveling: wondering

disregarded: neglected or overlooked
dulcet: soothing or pleasing
proceeding: continuing

resolutely: purposely
immobilized: frozen or not moving

Nate chuckled softly and planted one more kiss—a **delicate**, sweet one—on her puckered lips. "It's six-thirty," he repeated. "You have to get going."

"I don't want to go anywhere," Kristen said, her eyes still shut. "I want to stay right here."

"Uh-uh," Nate told her. "You get home late your first morning free and you'll be grounded again before I get a chance to ask you out."

Grudgingly, Kristen opened her eyes. "You're right," she said. "I have to get going." She stared into Nate's brown eyes for another moment, then got ready to get out and head to her dad's.

"Wait," Nate said. "You have an eyelash." He reached out with his index finger and removed the lash from her cheek, holding it out in front of her. "Make a wish." "I wish I could start every morning this way," she said. Then she blew the lash away.

Nate checked his thumb to make sure she had blown the lash free, and sure enough, it was gone. Then he grinned at Kristen. "So, tomorrow morning . . . what time should I pick you up?"

---

delicate: faint or subtle

Chapter Fifteen

At dawn the next day, Kristen was standing just inside the door to her mom's apartment when Nate's orange Volvo pulled up to the curb. Her heart jumped, and she realized a part of her was surprised to see him, even though he'd said he would be there. Maybe she'd just become **accustomed** to being let down.

"Morning," she breathed as she hopped into the passenger seat.

"Morning," Nate said with a grin. Then he piled a cardboard tray with two cups of coffee and a paper bag onto her lap.

"What's all this?" Kristen asked.

"Surfing provisions," Nate replied. "Take a look."

Kristen balanced the tray with the coffees on her knees and unrolled the top of the paper sack. "Nate—you didn't have to bring all of this." Kristen **scavenged** through the contents, discovering a box of doughnuts, a small bakery bag containing poppy-seed muffins, three bananas, an apple, an orange, and a couple of energy bars.

"I wasn't sure what you liked, so I wanted to have a good variety."

"I like everything in here," Kristen said, still staring into the bag.

"Good. Then we can save the leftovers for tomorrow."

Kristen gawked. "Tomorrow?"

"Well, yeah," Nate said. "I mean, unless you don't want me to pick you up."

"Oh, no—I mean, *yes*, of course I do," Kristen gushed. "I just figured that after you'd gotten up at four-thirty once, you'd want to avoid it again at all costs."

---

accustomed: familiarized   scavenged: searched

Nate placed one palm over his mouth to cover a **lethargic** yawn. "It's not that bad," he said. "But I could use a sip of that coffee," he added, gesturing toward the tray.

By the time they got to the Reach, it was five thirty-five and the sun had begun its **languorous ascent** into the sky. They'd made a quick stop at Kristen's father's house to grab her surfboard and gear, which her father had **beneficently** placed in the foyer as Kristen had requested of him when she'd phoned the previous night.

Her father had inquired as to how she would be getting there in the morning, and Kristen had almost told him, but at the last minute she decided to **refrain**. She didn't need her parents asking **intrusive** questions about Nate, especially when she barely even knew what to make of the whole thing. Neither one of them would be awake to see who she was really riding with, so instead she'd told them that Leah would be giving her a ride. It wouldn't hurt to let them think her relationship with Leah was still **amicable**. She could even tell her dad Leah was getting up early to run on the beach as training for basketball. He certainly wouldn't question Leah's **dedication** to the sport at which he thought she **excelled**.

Kristen changed into her gear in the back of Nate's car while he listened to music and drummed on the steering wheel. When she was ready, Nate helped her **convey** everything down to the shoreline, where she scurried into the water while he **retreated** to keep from getting splashed.

A couple of times, while Kristen was waiting in the lineup—for once, there were two other surfers out—she gazed back toward shore to see Nate sitting on a piece of driftwood with his coffee and what looked like a sketchbook. And more than once, toward the end of a ride, she managed to make eye contact with him and wave before wiping out.

In the past, Kristen had always **regarded** surfing as a solitary **pursuit**, and as she fought to find her balance and **maintain** it on

---

lethargic: sluggish	**refrain**: stop	**retreated**: withdrew
languorous: weary or listless	**intrusive**: prying	**regarded**: considered
ascent: rising or climb	**amicable**: friendly	**pursuit**: activity
beneficently: generously or kindly	**dedication**: commitment	**maintain**: hold
	excelled: stood out	
	convey: carry	

wave after wave, she still believed it to be true. But she had to admit, there was something soothing about looking up and seeing Nate sitting there on the beach. It was comforting to know that this time, when the waves brought her back to shore, there would be someone there waiting.

* * * * *

"The waves were better today," Nate said, making a left turn out of Kristen's mom's apartment complex. After Kristen had finished surfing, they'd driven back to town to drop off her gear and head to school. It made sense to keep everything at her mom's for now—even though her mother had had a fit about her "**gargantuan** board taking up half the hallway"—because Nate was planning to pick her up again on Friday.

Kristen took a sip of the coffee he'd brought her. Thanks to the **insulated** cozy cup he'd placed it in while she was surfing, it was still lukewarm. "Yeah, they were. You could tell?"

"Oh, yeah—big difference from yesterday," Nate said. He took a bite of his jelly doughnut and wiped the sugar off his lips with his sleeve. "Yesterday they looked all broken up—like lots of little waves instead of big, **continuous** ones, you know?"

Kristen nodded. "Choppy," she said. "That's the term for those conditions."

"So what's today called?" Nate asked. "It looked pretty perfect out there."

"Today it was glassy," Kristen said. "And clean. There wasn't much wind, and it came from offshore, which only helps to make the waves bigger." She took another sip of her coffee. "I asked Ken—he was the really tall guy in the black suit with orange stripes down the side?" Nate nodded. "And he said these conditions are supposed to stay with us for a while."

---

gargantuan: gigantic   **insulated:** protected   **continuous:** uninterrupted

"Cool," Nate said. "So I'll keep picking you up in the morning, and all this food won't go to waste."

"I wouldn't go that far," Kristen said, surveying the mess around her—a half a box of doughnuts on the floor, five muffins still in the bag, two more bananas. There was no **scarcity** of snacks. "You went a little overboard."

Nate shrugged. "Better safe than sorry."

One more sip of coffee drained Kristen's cup, so she reached into the backseat for the plastic grocery bag that had become their garbage **repository**. As she was replacing it behind Nate's seat, a small spiral-bound book caught her eye.

"Is this a journal or something?" she asked, picking it up.

Nate glanced at the notepad in her hand. "Sketchbook," he said.

"Can I look?" Kristen asked.

He stiffened. "I'm really not that good," he said. "I don't know if you want to—"

"Please?"

"Okay, I guess," he **relented**, not looking too thrilled about it. "But that's a pretty new one, so there's not a lot in there."

Kristen flipped the cover open and studied the drawings inside. Some of them were in charcoal, but most were done in pencil, including the one he'd obviously been working on this morning. "Is this . . . *me*?" Kristen asked, taking in a sketch of a surfer riding the lip of a wave with the sun rising in the distance.

"Yeah, but it's not done," Nate said quickly. "I couldn't get the angles right, and the light is coming from three different directions. Plus, I'm not great at people, so it's kind of—"

"It's amazing," Kristen said, still staring at it. The waves breaking on the shore, the white water, the rocks, the **vastness** of the ocean behind her—he'd managed to capture it all and make it look so real, in less than forty-five minutes.

Nate's ears reddened. "Thanks," he mumbled.

---

scarcity: shortage
repository: container

relented: yielded or conceded

vastness: enormity or size

"I mean it," Kristen said, glancing over at him. "It's really incredible. You're so talented."

"I don't know about that," Nate said.

"Well *I* do," Kristen replied. "I certainly can't draw like this—I don't know anyone who can." She flipped back through the rest of his drawings—trees, mountains, fields of tall grass and wildflowers. "So I guess when you told Dr. Griffin that you paint to relieve stress, you weren't talking about fences, huh?"

Nate chuckled. "No, I paint pictures. But really, I'm not that great. I just do it because . . . I don't know—because I need to, I guess."

Kristen nodded. "I know what you mean," she said. "That's why I surf. All that stuff I said in group about it being challenging and everything? I meant it, but really, when it comes down to it, I surf because I don't know what I'd do if I didn't. I love it, you know? It's like the only time I really feel at home."

"Yeah," Nate agreed. "That's what painting is like for me. And drawing. Any kind of art, really. I just get this urge to make stuff and I have to do it."

"It's a **compulsion**," Kristen said.

"Exactly."

"So then why don't you take any art classes?" Kristen asked.

Nate furrowed his brow. "I do."

"You do?" Kristen asked. "But I thought you were in the voc program—auto **mechanics**, carpentry, plumbing, **masonry**—that kind of stuff."

Nate laughed. "I *am* in the voc program, but it's not all stuff like that. The classes I take are mostly computer classes—graphic design, CAD, basic architecture and drafting."

"Wow, I didn't even know those things were available."

"Most people don't. They assume kids get on the **vocational** track because they're too dumb for traditional college prep classes."

---

compulsion: irresistible urge   **masonry:** stone or brickwork   **vocational:** professional
mechanics: method of   trade
routine operation

"I didn't think *that*," Kristen said. "I just thought—"

"Oh, I know," Nate assured her. "I wasn't **criticizing** you or anything. It's just that most people don't see tech classes as a valid choice—they think they're a last resort."

Kristen contemplated what he'd said and realized that he was right. She and her friends had always talked about the voc kids like they weren't **intellectual** enough to cut it in what they referred to as "regular" classes—like they were **inferior** in some way. But here was Nate—**unequivocally cerebral**, artistically gifted, and on the voc track.

"Do you think you'll go to college?" Kristen asked.

"I don't know," Nate replied. "Eventually, probably—but not right after high school. I want to take some time off and travel, see the world. Maybe do AmeriCorps or volunteer with some kind of overseas organization."

"What do your parents think about that?" Kristen asked.

Nate shrugged. "My dad's not so **keen** on the idea, but my mom's down with it. I think she knows that traditional education isn't really my thing—that I need a little more autonomy. That's why she cuts me so much **slack**."

Kristen thought back to the night when she'd seen Nate and his mom at the police station. True, his mother had seemed upset, but not so much with Nate as with the situation. "That's kind of cool."

"What?" Nate asked.

"That your mom gets you," Kristen said. She wasn't sure she'd ever met anyone who understood her **implicitly**. It seemed that she was always on the outside of things—standing on the sideline and never quite finding the right time or place to enter the game.

"I guess it is," Nate said. "She gets on my case a lot—"

"When you spray-paint the school?" Kristen asked.

"Yeah," Nate chuckled. "But for the most part, she lets me be who I am."

---

criticizing: judging or condemning
intellectual: intelligent
inferior: mediocre or substandard

unequivocally: clearly or plainly
cerebral: intelligent or brainy

keen: enthusiastic
slack: moderation
implicitly: totally

Kristen smiled. It sounded so nice—the **notion** of being under-stood and accepted. She wasn't even sure if she knew what being herself **entailed**.

"So is that why you're in group?" Kristen asked. "Because of the spray-paint **incident**?"

Nate shook his head. "No, I've been hanging with Mr. G. for a while now. It's cool, though. He's a good guy."

Kristen waited, hoping that Nate would explain or at least offer a few more details, but he didn't. She watched him drive for a while, studying his sharp jawline, his angular **profile**, his intense eyes. He seemed so **cogent**, so **lucid**, so . . . healthy. What was he doing in therapy? Why did he need it, aside from the fact that he was a little **unconventional**, with his black attire and his **refusal** to **conform**?

As she watched, Nate made the turn into Adams High, heading down the tree-lined drive that led to the student parking area. "What about you?" he asked. "How did you end up with Mr. G.?"

Kristen stared through the pine needles at the brick building **looming** in the distance. It was getting closer by the second—far too quickly for her to explain Dr. Griffin's **theory** of connectivity and why he thought she would **benefit** from group psychotherapy. "Just trying to meet new people," she said.

Nate smirked. "Met anyone interesting yet?" he asked, turning into the student parking lot and cruising to the back row.

"A pregnant chick and a guy who only wears black," she said.

"Yeah? And what do you think?"

Kristen shrugged. "They're okay," she said as Nate pulled into a space.

He shifted his car into first and pulled up the emergency brake, then turned to her. "Okay?" he asked, his eyebrows arched upward.

Kristen tried to keep a straight face, but it was futile. She didn't seem **capable** of looking into Nate's eyes without smiling. "More

notion: idea	**profile:** outline	**conform:** fit in
entailed: involved or required	**cogent:** convincing	**looming:** emerging
incident: occurrence or episode	**lucid:** sane	**theory:** doctrine or view
	unconventional: unusual	**benefit:** profit
	refusal: rejection	**capable:** able

than okay," she said quietly, and for once, Nate was the first one to look away.

"Hey," Kristen said, changing the subject. "Do you think maybe I could see some of your paintings sometime?"

"There's not much to see," Nate said, "but sure. How about Friday night?"

Kristen's heart jumped into her throat. "Friday night?"

"Yeah," Nate said. "I could pick you up, we could . . . I don't know, get dinner? See a movie? Something like that. And then you could come over and I could show you some of the stuff I've done."

"Really?" Kristen asked.

"Sure. I've seen you in your **element**. It's only fair that I let you see me in mine."

Kristen grinned. *In my element,* she thought. *I like that.* That was exactly how surfing felt to her—like she was where she was meant to be, doing what she was meant to do.

"What do you say?" Nate asked.

What could she say? "Yes—I mean, that sounds fun. What time?"

"Five? Six?" Nate ventured. "I don't know. We can **finalize** the details tomorrow morning."

"Tomorrow morning?" Kristen asked.

"Yeah, when I pick you up to go surfing."

"Oh, right," Kristen said, amazed at how easily everything was falling into place. Her grin stretched so widely across her face that it seemed to be knocking her ears into new positions. "Well," she said, undoing her seat belt, "I guess we should probably head inside."

"Yeah," Nate nodded. "We probably should. But . . ." He paused to undo his seat belt and turn toward Kristen. "I thought maybe . . ."

"Maybe what?" Kristen asked. She crossed her left leg underneath herself so that she could turn to face him.

---

element: domain or territory   finalize: settle

"Maybe," Nate breathed, leaning toward her, "I could just"—he put his arm behind her neck and gently pulled her closer—"kiss you again. Just for a minute."

"I think that could be arranged," Kristen breathed as her mouth neared his, and then—

"Oh my God!" someone exclaimed from outside the car. "I told you she was a sex addict!"

Kristen bolted upright.

"Talk about slumming—she must be really hard up!"

"Ignore them," Nate said, but it was too late. Kristen was already miserably **fixated** on the scene outside the car. At some point, while she'd been **mesmerized** by Nate's dark eyes and the possibility of kissing him again, Tracy, Luke, Leah, and Trevor had gathered next to her window.

"Whoa," Trevor yelled. "I knew she liked it, but I had no idea she'd sink so low to get more. Careful you don't **contract** any diseases from her, Nate!"

Kristen gaped at her former friends, stunned by their cruelty and **aghast** at being **besieged** in front of Nate. She surveyed their faces in turn—Tracy, Luke, Leah, Trevor. They were all laughing like they were watching a sitcom in progress. How could they treat her like this? How could they have turned on her so quickly? Had they *ever* been her friends in the first place?

Horrified, she turned to Nate. "I'm sorry. I didn't mean to get you involved in this. They're—"

"Stop it, Kristen," Nate said. He gazed straight into her eyes, seemingly **oblivious** to the hooting and howling going on just outside his car. "I don't care what they say, and neither should you."

"I know," Kristen said, staring down at her hands, which she was **wringing** in her lap. "I just—"

"Doing it in the parking lot! You better be careful, Kristen," came Tracy's voice again, "or you'll end up like your friend Preggy Sue."

---

fixated: focused	**aghast**: shocked	**oblivious**: unmindful
mesmerized: hypnotized	**besieged**: attacked	**wringing**: squeezing
contract: catch	**horrified**: shocked or dismayed	

Kristen took a deep, shuddering breath and tried to figure out what to do.

"It's okay," Nate said. He put his hand on Kristen's thigh in an attempt to **ameliorate** her **anxiety**, but that only **elicited** more laughter from Tracy and her posse.

"I guess they don't care who's watching," Trevor cried, **provoking** another cackle from Tracy. Kristen did notice, however, that Luke and Leah weren't **contributing** to the **revelry**.

"Come on, let's go inside," Leah said. "I'm getting cold."

"Maybe you should hop in with Kristen," Trevor suggested. "It looks plenty hot in there."

Again, Tracy laughed, but Luke and Leah had started toward the school, so she and Trevor, accustomed to traveling in herds, followed suit. When they were gone, Kristen shook her head. "I'm really sorry, Nate," she said, staring at her lap. "It's me they're making fun of, you know. Not you."

"I'm not upset, Kristen," Nate replied. "They're jerks—it's not exactly news to me."

"Yeah, but—"

Nate placed his hand on Kristen's chin and tried to angle her head upward, but she couldn't meet his eyes.

"We're going to be late," she said, grabbing her backpack from the floor.

"We still have five minutes," Nate protested, but Kristen couldn't stand to sit there with him any longer. She opened her door and fled toward the school, being careful to make a wide loop so she could enter through the side door, thereby avoiding Tracy and her gang.

"Kristen, wait!" she heard Nate calling in the distance, but she wasn't about to stop. He claimed to be **impervious** to all of the **taunts**, but for how long would he honestly want to be involved with the **licentious** laughingstock of the school? How many **barbs** would it take before he saw what everybody else saw—that she wasn't

---

ameliorate: improve	**contributing:** adding	**licentious:** promiscuous or
anxiety: uneasiness	**revelry:** merriment	immoral
elicited: brought out	**impervious:** unaffected	**barbs:** wisecracks
provoking: prompting	**taunts:** insults	

worth his time? Chances were, not many, but Kristen didn't intend to hang around long enough to find out.

$$* \quad * \quad * \quad * \quad *$$

"Kristen!" Macy called as Kristen rushed down the hall. She'd managed to **evade** Macy and Nate all day, skipping lunch and hanging out in the girls' bathroom with one of the stall doors locked. But now, just when she'd been almost home free, Macy had managed to spot her.

Ducking a little lower and trying to blend into the crowd, Kristen kept walking, hoping to lose Macy somewhere en route to the bus. It wouldn't have been too hard, considering the fact that Macy had begun to waddle more than walk, but unfortunately, Nate was with her, and he managed to weave through the crowd, catching up to Kristen just outside the main entrance.

"Hey—where were you at lunch? Macy and I looked all over for you," he said, falling into step next to her.

Kristen glanced left and right, half expecting jeers and sneers from both directions, but it seemed that she had somehow lucked out and settled into a crowd of students from the lower **echelons** of the popularity pyramid—kids who either didn't understand what a **pariah** she was or who still considered themselves **substandard** in comparison.

"I, um, had to retake a French test," Kristen lied.

"Oh," Nate said.

"Hey! Wait up," Macy called, and as Nate was right next to her, this time Kristen couldn't pretend not to have heard. "Sheesh—you're in a hurry," she commented when she'd reached them. "What's up?"

"I have to get home," Kristen said. "My mom has a thing—at the station," she added quickly, "and she wants me to attend."

---

evade: avoid
echelons: levels

pariah: outcast

substandard: inferior or mediocre

"Too bad," Macy said. "Nate and I were going to see if you wanted to hang out, maybe go bowling or something—candlepin, of course. Those big balls are too heavy for me these days."

Kristen was touched that they were trying so hard to reach out to her, but they'd really have a better time on their own anyway. And they'd be less likely to **incur derision**. "That sounds like fun," she said. "Maybe another time."

Just then, the bus pulled up and students started to board. "I have to go," Kristen said. She started to turn, but Nate grabbed her shoulder.

"I can give you a ride," he offered.

"Thanks, but I have to hurry," Kristen said.

"I could go straight there," Nate told her. "You'd get home faster than you will riding the bus."

He was right, Kristen knew, but she couldn't bear to face him after everything that had been said about her this morning. He obviously just felt sorry for her, and she didn't need his pity. "That's okay," she said. "My mom's expecting me on the bus—I better just stick to the plan."

As she hurried toward the bus and joined the line of students waiting to board, she knew that Macy and Nate were probably staring after her, but she didn't want to look back. If they hadn't already figured out what a **liability** she was, they would soon enough, and then they'd be glad to be **divested** of her presence and all the baggage that came with it.

*   *   *   *   *

When the bus finally arrived at Kristen's stop, she shambled to the front and **disembarked** along with the seven other kids who got off at Riverside. The others chatted as they walked, but Kristen kept to herself. She glanced up at the bus driver, waiting to be waved

---

incur: undergoing or facing **liability:** burden   **disembarked:** left
derision: ridicule   **divested:** rid or freed

across, but when she finally got the all-clear signal, something across the street stopped her dead in her tracks—her father's car.

The bus driver tapped the horn, awakening Kristen from her daze, and she headed toward the black BMW, wondering, with a growing sense of dread in her stomach, what he was doing here.

"Kristen," her father said, beaming as he stood to greet her, his gray slacks **billowing** in the wind. He spread his arms as if waiting to embrace her—a gesture completely **foreign** to his **repertoire** as far as Kristen could recall.

She furrowed her brow and stared at him. "What's going on?" she asked.

"What's going on?" her father said with a laugh. "Does there have to be something going on for me to want to see my little girl?"

Little girl? Kristen thought, her pulse speeding up. What had gotten into him?

"All right," Mr. Carmichael said, "I'll admit it—I *am* here for a special reason. Why don't you hop in so we can talk?" he suggested, pressing a button that popped his trunk. "Oops," he said, pressing his key fob again. This time the **interior** light came on, and Kristen heard all of the doors unlock. "There we go," Mr. Carmichael said. "Hop in."

"Can't you just tell me out here?" Kristen said.

Her father blinked a few times. "Well, I guess I could," he said.

"Well? What is it?"

Mr. Carmichael cleared his throat. "All right," he said. "This isn't exactly how I wanted to tell you, but . . . last night I proposed to Carrie. We're getting married!" He stretched his arms out again, but only slightly this time so that if Kristen didn't jump into them for a hug, he wouldn't be left standing there looking stupid.

"You're what?" Kristen asked. She was in no mood for a hug.

"Carrie and I are getting married," Mr. Carmichael repeated.

---

billowing: waving   **repertoire:** list of skills or   **interior:** inside
foreign: uncharacteristic   behaviors

Kristen stared at him until his smile faded. Then she walked around his car and straight into her mother's apartment, where she slammed the door and locked it.

Chapter Sixteen

"I understand that it's all a little surprising," Kristen's mother said, plunking down a plate of fried chicken—fresh from the convenience store down the road. "But Kristen, you really can't just walk away from your father like that."

Kristen shook her head. Why couldn't she? Why was it that she was the only member of her family who couldn't do whatever she wanted, whenever she wanted, without having to answer for any of it? It was bad enough having Carrie around once a week—Kristen couldn't stand the idea of having her there every single time she visited her father. And she wouldn't even be visiting her father anymore. Once they were married, she'd be visiting her father *and* Carrie. Carrie would be her stepmother! Suddenly all those Disney films were beginning to make sense.

"This marriage is going to be a good thing for you too, you know," Ms. Graham continued, spooning out day-old convenience store coleslaw and offering the Styrofoam tub to Kristen.

"No, thanks," Kristen said. She poked the drumstick on her plate with her fork, and a piece of overcooked extracrispy coating flaked off. Why was her mom standing up for her dad, anyway? Usually she jumped at the chance to criticize him.

"Carrie's house is much larger than your father's," Kristen's mom went on. "You'll have your own bedroom *and* bathroom there, plus it's right in town, so you won't have to commute back and forth so far with your father."

Kristen scrunched her eyebrows together. "What do you mean?"

"Well, once your father sells the house on the beach—which shouldn't take long, considering the current real estate market—

you won't have to travel forty-five minutes to see him. Carrie is only about ten minutes away from here, which means—"

"Wait a second," Kristen interrupted, sitting up. "What do you mean, 'once dad sells the house on the beach'?"

Kristen's mother stiffened. "He didn't tell you?"

"Tell me what?" Kristen demanded.

"Oh, honey—I'm sorry. I thought he'd already discussed his plans with you. I guess you just didn't give him a chance to explain."

"What are you talking about, Mom? What's going on?"

Ms. Graham set down her fork and wiped her hands on her napkin, folding it neatly and setting it next to her plate. "I'm not sure I should get into this right now," she said.

"It's a little late," Kristen retorted. "You already are, so you might as well just tell me everything."

"All right," Ms. Graham said. "I suppose you're right. Your father is putting his house on the market and moving in with Carrie."

"He's what? Why?"

"Because it doesn't make sense—**financially** or **logistically**—for them to have two separate houses anymore, and Carrie's is bigger. Plus, it's closer to your father's work and to your school—it just makes more sense."

"And just when was he planning to tell me about this?" Kristen barked.

"I'm sure he **intended** to tell you soon," Ms. Graham replied, "if you would just give him a chance. Believe me, I am *not* a fan of this woman, Kristen, and I don't know what's gotten into your father's head. But this is the way things are, and we're all trying to do what's best for you here. Can't you at least try and understand that instead of giving us so much trouble every step of the way?"

Kristen shook her head, stunned that her mom would turn this around on her. How could her dad have made such a big decision without even telling her? Not only was he getting married, but he

---

financially: monetarily   **logistically:** provisioning supplies and services   **intended:** meant or planned

was selling his house—the house he'd always said was her house too. So much for that theory.

"Oh, Kristen," Ms. Graham said as Kristen slumped back in her chair and folded her arms across her chest. "Try to remember— things change, and change isn't **necessarily** a bad thing. In fact, most of the time it's **positive**. For instance, I'm in line for a **promotion** at the station. They're considering me for a regular anchor position on the six o'clock news—*weekdays*."

The way her mother said it, anyone would have thought she'd been elected to the presidency.

"If I get it, it will mean a lot of additional hours during the week—even a few extra nights, which on the one hand could be **taxing**, but on the other hand, it will give you a lot more time to spend with your dad. And I think that's important."

Aha—the real **motivation** for her mother's **unprecedented** display of support for Mr. Carmichael. Kristen could hardly believe what she was hearing. Her father was getting married, her mother was adding more hours to her work schedule, the beach house was a thing of the past, she was going to be spending more time with her dad and his **insipid** girlfriend. They were making plans left and right, and she was hearing about them all at the last minute, like she was some kind of **spectator** and not someone whose life was going to be **affected**.

Had they forgotten she was their daughter, or did they just not care?

Judging from their **prior** track record, Kristen was **inclined** to believe the **latter**.

---

necessarily: inevitably or certainly
positive: good or beneficial
promotion: advancement
taxing: exhausting
motivation: incentive

unprecedented: novel or new
insipid: dull
spectator: onlooker
affected: touched
prior: earlier

inclined: tending or predisposed
latter: second-mentioned of two

Chapter Seventeen

Kristen watched as the glowing red numbers on her alarm clock counted off the night hours: 1 A.M., 2 A.M., 3 A.M.—she was awake to see each of them arrive and depart. By 4 A.M., she'd had enough.

Creeping down the stairs to the dining room, she removed her mother's car keys from the hook by the door, and, with her wet suit on and the rest of her gear stuffed into her duffel, she procured her surfboard from the hallway—her mother would be glad to see it gone—and headed out into the darkness.

By the time she arrived at the beach, it was nearly five. The sun wasn't up yet, but there was enough light for her to navigate her way down to the rocks and put on the rest of her gear.

"It's too much," she muttered to herself as she slid her feet into her booties. "It's all too much." School, the rumors, Tracy, Trevor. She was completely alone. Whom did she have in her life? Her parents? Yeah, right. Uncle Pete, but he was so far away. Most of the people she knew wouldn't miss her at all if she was gone. And anyone who thought they missed her, like Nate or Macy, would soon realize they were better off without her.

Nate was a smart guy—he had a future. And so did Macy. She was making all the right decisions, and she was strong enough to **withstand** the ridicule, strong enough not to care. "But I'm not," Kristen thought. She was weak and she knew it, and she **detested** herself for it.

For nearly two years now, Kristen had felt her life spiraling out of control. First her friends had changed and left her behind, then Pete had moved. Then her parents had divorced, and school had

---

withstand: endure   **detested:** hated

started to feel like a prison. She'd been alone and **fraught** with pain for so long, she couldn't even remember what life had felt like before. As she put on her gloves and hood, she watched the waves rolling and breaking and knew that all she needed to do was get out there in the ocean—the only place she'd ever felt at home.

When Kristen had all of her gear on, she walked into the water, carrying her board until she could float it. Then, when the water was just over waist height, she climbed onto her board and began to paddle out. The conditions were still ideal, just as Ken had said they would be, and the swell looked to be somewhere around four or five feet. With such **idyllic circumstances**, there would likely be more surfers coming soon, Kristen realized. She'd better get out there fast, before she had to share the ocean with anyone.

In less than ten minutes, Kristen had managed to line herself up for her first approach, and she couldn't have asked for a better wave. At least five feet at its peak, there was nothing mushy about it. When she popped up, she found herself right on the shoulder, **accelerating** quickly but holding steady, perfectly balanced. There was no wind today—not a single bump in the water, and as Kristen crouched on her board, she felt a sense of **equilibrium** she'd never encountered before.

Keeping her weight low, she cross-stepped once and then again, until eventually she had one foot on the nose—hanging five—and her second foot ready to step. Focusing her weight and her energy deep into her heels, she placed her left foot on the nose of her board so that all ten of her toes gripped the edge, and then, with a deep inhalation, she extended both of her arms.

Uncle Pete had been right—noseriding was an incredible feeling, like nothing else Kristen had ever experienced. She felt like she was flying—gliding across the top of the water, **propelled** by nothing but the **supreme** power of the ocean—and she knew, somewhere deep within her soul, that this was the ocean's way of

---

fraught: filled
idyllic: peaceful or heavenly
circumstances: surroundings

accelerating: increasing speed
equilibrium: balance or composure

propelled: moved
supreme: ultimate

welcoming her. Before the wave brought her too far in, and before it broke on her, Kristen took a look at the sun, which was now rising, then went down.

At first, the water held her under, a **phenomenon** to which Kristen was **habituated**. She'd been held under plenty of times, and she'd learned not to fight it but instead to wait and then make her way to the surface when the wave had passed. Some part of her was always tempted to just give herself over to the ocean **unreservedly**—become part of it—but the desire was fleeting.

After a few moments under, her instincts kicked in like usual and her body screamed for air. She started to push her way up, but something was wrong. The pressure was too intense, and she couldn't seem to get the right angle.

Gasping, she inhaled a mouthful of water, which her lungs attempted to reject. What was happening? No, this wasn't possible—she couldn't be drowning. She was an experienced surfer. She knew how to take on a wave that size. But even as her mind raced with these thoughts, she felt herself being sucked in deeper. Her body was fighting—arms flailing, legs kicking, stomach and throat trying to **expel** the liquid that was coming in—but inside, Kristen started to **succumb**. She was tired of fighting, so tired. She bobbed to the surface **momentarily**, choking and craving air, but the more she coughed and wheezed, the more water her body took in. The ocean was filling her body, **seeping** into her lungs, and little by little, her body was **relenting**. Soon it would occupy all the spaces where pain had lived for so long and **eradicate** it from her being forever.

She bobbed to the surface one more time—at least, it seemed that she did. Everything grew lighter for a moment, as though someone had opened a window shade in a dark room, but a second later she felt the **density** of the water around her once again, **attesting** that her **liberation** was almost complete. And then everything went black.

phenomenon: experience	**succumb:** yield or surrender	**eradicate:** remove
habituated: accustomed	**momentarily:** briefly	**density:** mass
unreservedly: entirely	**seeping:** oozing	**attesting:** confirming
expel: eject	**relenting:** surrendering	**liberation:** deliverance

Chapter Eighteen

When she opened her eyes, the light was blinding. She tried to speak, but all that came out was a weak rasp.

"Kristen?"

Squinting, Kristen gazed at the dark shape before her. She knew this person. He was familiar, but the light was so bright behind him.

"Kristen—are you awake?"

"Nate?" she said, but her voice sounded more like the wheeze of someone suffering from **pronounced** emphysema than her own. "Why is my voice so scratchy?" she rasped.

"They had to intubate you," Nate said. Then he took a few steps toward the door and said, "Excuse me, nurse? She's awake again."

Intu-what? Nurse? Kristen lay there as another figure—a smaller one this time, and easier to see because she was dressed in white—approached. She shined a penlight in Kristen's eyes, holding them open with her thumb and forefinger.

"Still looks good," she commented. "I'm just going to take your blood pressure again." Kristen felt something tightening around her upper arm and then releasing with a faint whistling sound. "One-twenty over sixty," the nurse said. "Everything seems fine," she added with a smile. "I'll let the doctor know you're awake, dear. She'll be in to see you when she finishes her other rounds."

"Thanks," Nate said as the nurse left the room. Then he returned to Kristen's side. "How do you feel?" he asked.

Kristen brought her hand to her throat, which was extremely sore, and shook her head and winced in answer. Conserving words seemed **imperative**. "What happened?" she mouthed.

---

pronounced: unmistakable **imperative:** necessary

"You went surfing and you went under. You almost drowned," Nate told her point-blank, and suddenly the events of the morning came back to her. The perfect wave, noseriding, going under and feeling the ocean **obliterate** every part of her being. It had been terrifying, but strangely peaceful, too.

"Who—?" Kristen started, but a coughing fit took over. When she finally stopped, Nate put his finger to his lips and shushed her.

"I did," he said. "I pulled you out of the water and your mom called 911."

Kristen shook her head and squinted, and Nate seemed to understand. "I went to your mom's to pick you up this morning," he explained. "You were kind of terse yesterday, but I figured you'd still want to surf today. But you had already left. She said your surfboard was gone and all your gear too, so we figured you'd headed to the beach. Your mom was pretty pissed that you didn't leave a note or anything, but I told her I was heading out to meet you and that I'd make sure you got her car back to her right away."

Figures, Kristen thought. *She was more concerned about her stupid car than she was about me.*

"She was worried, though, Kristen," Nate said, as though reading her mind. "She insisted on coming with me to make sure everything was okay—said you were upset about your father getting married or something?"

Kristen pressed her eyes closed and nodded. She didn't want to think about that right now. She didn't want to think about any of it. But Nate kept going.

"So anyway, we headed to the beach and saw your mom's car in the parking lot, and when we walked down to the beach, we saw you—surfing, standing on the very end of your board with your arms out. You looked like a bird, Kristen—like a beautiful, graceful bird. And then you went down."

---

obliterate: destroy

As Nate related the events of the morning from his perspective, Kristen felt like she was reliving it all over again—getting up, taking the car keys, driving to the beach, putting on her gear, getting into the water. But this time, she seemed to be having a more intense reaction to it all, whereas the first time—when she'd actually been living it—she had felt more like she was watching everything unfold from somewhere outside of her body. It had been as though she were an **automaton**, acting without feeling or emotion.

"Kristen," Nate said, his voice cracking. "I've seen you surf, and I've seen you wipe out, but what I saw today—that wasn't an accident, was it?"

Kristen looked into Nate's eyes—his incredibly clear, deep brown eyes—and felt like everything inside of her was coming **unraveled**. Suddenly, all of the emotion that had been building up for the last few weeks—for the last two years—was too much. She felt the weight of it all like a physical lump in her body, spreading into every limb.

Her chest tightened, and her shoulders began to tremble. When she gasped for breath, her whole body shuddered and her throat felt like it was **constricting** involuntarily. Her mouth quivered, and then finally, the tears that had begun to well up in her eyes started spilling down her face.

Kristen sat up and hunched forward, wrapping her arms around her body and sobbing. She felt so empty and alone and confused and hurt. And even though she felt a little safer when Nate encircled her with his arms, she still couldn't help feeling that things were never going to get any better.

"I know what it's like, Kristen," Nate said, and Kristen began to sob even harder. "You feel helpless and hopeless and worthless, and you don't think that's ever going to change, but it will."

"No, it won't," Kristen said, her voice a **hoarse** whisper. It took all the wind she could **muster** to force out even a small sound. "This

---

automaton: robot   constricting: tightening   muster: summon
unraveled: undone   hoarse: rough

is me," she said, wiping her nose on the white hospital bedsheet. "This is the way I am. I mean, it wasn't—it wasn't what you think, out there in the ocean. I really just got sucked down, and couldn't get up. But maybe some part of me really was trying to just surrender, give in. Because that's who I am—I'm weak."

"That's not true, Kristen," Nate said. "I've seen you—I've seen behind your eyes, and I know you're a beautiful person. And you don't have to feel this way. You can get help."

Kristen pulled back and looked at Nate through tear-clouded eyes. "Help?" she whispered. "What kind of help?"

"Like counseling," Nate said. "Or maybe even medicine—I don't know. But I do know that you can get through this, and you don't have to spend the rest of your life feeling so alone."

Kristen shook her head and wiped her eyes and nose again. "Great," she rasped. "You think I'm wacked."

"I don't think you're wacked, Kristen," Nate said. Then he took her chin in his palm and looked directly into her eyes. "I think you're depressed." Kristen tried to turn away, but Nate gently nudged her chin back so that she was still facing him. "A lot of the things you say sound like things my older brother used to say."

Kristen squinted. Nate had never mentioned an older brother. She'd always thought he was an only child.

"His name was Brian," Nate said.

Was?

"He killed himself when I was thirteen. Right before we moved to New Hampshire."

Kristen's mouth dropped open.

"I don't talk about him much," Nate went on. "But that's why I see Mr. G. My mom's **petrified** that I might get depressed too. All the black probably doesn't help," he said, glancing down at his T-shirt, "but I don't wear it to bug her. I just don't like thinking about clothes."

---

petrified: frightened

In **spite** of the fact that she was in a hospital bed, in spite of the fact that her throat ached worse than it had the one time she'd had strep, and in spite of the fact that she'd almost drowned that morning, Kristen cracked a smile.

"How old was he?" she whispered.

"Sixteen—same as you," Nate said. "And he didn't think anything would ever get better, either. But it could have if he'd given it a chance. I know it could have."

Kristen's lower lip began to tremble again, and just when she thought she'd cried all the moisture out of her body, a fresh round of tears sprang forth.

"It's okay," Nate said, holding her tightly and rubbing her back. "Go ahead and cry. I'll stay right here and hold you as long as want me to."

The sobbing lasted for a solid five minutes, and by the time Kristen felt cried out, Nate's T-shirt was **drenched**. "Sorry," she whispered as she pulled away, noticing the dark circle on his shoulder.

"Not a problem," Nate said. "I've got twelve more like it at home." Kristen sniffed, managing a weak smile, and Nate handed her a box of tissues from the bedside table. "Your mom and dad are here," he said, "but they went down to the cafeteria for coffee a while ago. With Mr. G."

"Dr. Griffin's here?" Kristen whispered.

Nate nodded. "Your parents called him. They're really concerned about you, Kristen." Kristen rolled her eyes. "I know you don't believe that, and maybe your relationships with them aren't great, but they do care—I can see it in their eyes. The doctor told them your were physically fine—breathing on your own, no sign of damage, et cetera—but they still wouldn't go for coffee with Mr. G. until I promised them I would stay right with you here the whole time. I'm not even allowed a pee break."

"You can go if you need to," Kristen offered.

---

spite: defiance or regardless **drenched:** soaked

He smiled. "I don't need to. And I don't *want* to leave you, either. I care about you, Kristen. So do your parents. And so do Macy and Mr. G. and a lot of other people."

Kristen looked into Nate's eyes, but she couldn't hold his gaze for long—it was too intense, and she was worried about what he'd see behind her eyes now. **Sorrow**? **Desperation**? She was sure it was all there, but she didn't want him to see any of it. She wanted to be a good person—a person worth knowing. Someone who could accept the **affection** he was offering her and be able to give some back.

"I heard Mr. G. say something about seeing him twice a week for a while—would you do that?" Nate asked.

Kristen raised her eyes and looked up at him through her lashes. And then she nodded.

Nate smiled. "You can do this, Kristen. I know you can. And I'm going to be right here for you to lean on anytime you need me—you understand that?" Again Kristen nodded. "Good," Nate said. "That's good." He wrapped his arms back around her and held her close. "You're going to be fine, you know," he told her, and in that moment, Kristen believed him.

Because sitting there in the hospital with Nate's arms around her, for the first time in a long time, Kristen felt at home somewhere else other than in the ocean.

---

sorrow: sadness   desperation: hopelessness   affection: love

"Do you want to take this one?" Dr. Griffin asked, glancing over at Kristen, who was settled into her usual spot on the bean-bag chair, flanked by Nate on one side and Alice Tartan on the other. Alice was occupying Macy's normal chair, since Macy was still recovering from giving birth to her baby the previous week.

Kristen smiled at Dr. Griffin, then turned to the shy blonde guy perched on the edge of the couch. "Hi Andy," she greeted him. "What Dr. G here wants me to say is that the first rule of the group is—"

"Man, she totally messed it up!" Mikey interrupted in an indignant whine.

Everyone but Andy laughed—even Dr. Griffin. But after a quick chuckle, Dr. G cleared his throat and **admonished** Mikey to let Kristen finish.

"Right, okay," Kristen began again, biting back a smirk. "The first rule of *Fight Club* is that we do not talk about . . ." She stopped as she recognized the same confused expression coming over Andy's features that she'd felt when she first heard those words. "Look, I'm sorry Mikey, but the joke's getting old," she said.

"Yeah, you know, it kind of is," Ellen Stank agreed, exchanging a light-hearted eye roll with Kristen.

"Fine, whatever," Mikey muttered.

Kristen returned her gaze to Andy. "Don't worry about any of that," she said, flashing what she hoped was a reassuring smile. "The important thing to know is, whatever we say in this room stays in this room. So you don't have to worry that anyone else will find out, okay?"

---

admonished: warned

Andy nodded, but he still looked nervous. Kristen couldn't help wondering what he was there for. Still, at least she knew that being in that room meant there was a really good chance he'd start feeling better soon from whatever was bugging him.

As Dr. Griffin launched into his whole "there is no rule number two" routine, Kristen leaned back and thought about how far she'd come since she was the one in the hot seat, looking around the room at all these people she barely knew. It hadn't seemed possible back then that she could ever be happy again, anywhere outside the ocean. And now . . .

"So, while we let Andy see what we're about here, does anyone want to share?" Dr. Griffin asked.

Kristen felt a gentle nudge on her left side, and glanced down to see Nate's elbow poking her. She narrowed her eyes at him, but he just raised his eyebrows encouragingly.

"I guess I will," Kristen reluctantly volunteered. She'd been having individual therapy sessions with Dr. Griffin ever since that morning when she'd nearly drowned, just like Nate had suggested, so she'd gotten way better at talking about her life these past couple of months. And she totally trusted everyone in this group. But still . . . she just wasn't the queen of exposing her private life to other people. Although, this was something she knew everyone would be happy to hear.

Kristen took a deep breath. "So, my mom took me shopping this weekend, for something to wear to my dad's wedding," she said.

Alice groaned. "Uh oh—this doesn't sound good," she said sympathetically.

"No, actually, it's okay," Kristen said. "I mean, we'd had it all planned, and then at the last minute Dave called and I was sure she was going to ditch me and go out with him. I even said it was fine, that I didn't need her to help me pick out a dress. But she told Dave she already had plans with me, and she'd have to see him later."

Dr. Griffin edged forward in his chair. "So what did that say to you?" he asked.

Kristen shrugged. "Well, at first I thought it was just a guilt thing. Like she's done a lot since I—you know," she finished awkwardly, with a glance at Andy. The new guy didn't need to hear about her near-death moment on his very first day, but the others would get what she meant. She looked at Ellen, who nodded at her to continue. "Anyway, ever since that whole thing, she's always trying to talk to me more, just like my dad. 'Checking in,' they call it. But when we were shopping for the dress, she wasn't just asking about me, or listening to my stuff. She kind of started to talk to me about how she was feeling, too, with the wedding coming up. How sad she feels about what happened to our family, that kind of thing. And how much she wants to make sure that no matter what, I can always be close to both of them. I felt like she—I don't know, like she needs me too."

Kristen stopped, suddenly self-conscious about how much she'd just blabbed. She looked instinctively at Nate, who gave her arm a supportive squeeze. He'd already heard the story, of course, which was why he'd pushed her to share it in group. He'd been so amazing—almost more excited than she was when her mom came through like that.

"That's great Kristen," Alice said. "I'm so happy for you."

A chorus of "yeah, me too"s went around the room, and Dr. Griffen just looked at her with a gleam of satisfied pride in his eyes.

"Oh, and I almost forgot," Kristen added. "I talked to Macy last night. She'd just woken up from sleeping for, like, *days*. She said she's never been so exhausted in her life, and she's also never seen so much—"

"I don't want to hear it," Mikey blurted out, holding his hands to his ears.

Kristen laughed. "Anyway, she wanted me to tell all of you hi, and thanks for the cards, and she's doing okay. A little sad, but she knows everything's for the best."

Kristen looked down at the floor as the group fell into an unusual silence, all of them probably feeling some of that sadness themselves. Going with Macy to her appointments, Kristen had even started to feel attached to the baby, and that was nothing compared to what Macy experienced during her pregnancy. Kristen couldn't imagine how hard it had to have been for Macy to say goodbye. But Macy really was convinced she'd done the right thing at least.

"Nate and I are stopping over there tonight, if any of you want me to pass on a message," Kristen finished.

"Thanks, Kristen," Dr. Griffin said. "I'm glad Macy's doing well." After a pause, he continued. "Anyone else want to talk?"

Kristen drifted off into her thoughts as Ellen started to tell a story about a fight with her sister. Alice jumped in after Ellen with some problems she was having with a friend, and then time was up. These days it seemed like the group sessions just flew by.

"So hey, that wasn't so bad, was it?" Nate asked as he and Kristen stood. He slung his arm over her shoulder as they walked out, then as soon as they reached the hallway he reached down and slipped his hand around hers, the way he always did.

"Okay, it was fine," Kristen relented. "But remember the deal . . ."

"Oh come on, are you serious?" Nate protested.

Kristen grinned at him. "I shared a cheesy story in group," she said. "Now *you* have to show up tomorrow wearing something that's not black."

"Does dark gray count?"

Kristen laughed. "I don't know . . ."

Before she could go on, Nate pulled her to the side of the hall-way and held her close, leaning down to kiss her. It was perfect, as perfect as every kiss with Nate was—leaving every inch of her tingling. "I think we can work something out," she teased.

TEST PREPARATION
GUIDES

The SparkNotes team figured it was time to cut standardized tests down to size. We've studied the tests for you, so that SparkNotes test prep guides are:

SMARTER
Packed with critical-thinking skills and test-
taking strategies that will improve your score.

BETTER
Fully up to date, covering all new features of the tests,
with study tips on every type of question.

FASTER
Our books cover exactly what you need to
know for the test. No more, no less.

SparkNotes The New SAT—Deluxe Internet Edition
SparkNotes The New ACT—Deluxe Internet Edition
SparkNotes SAT Verbal Workbook
SparkNotes SAT Math Workbook
SparkNotes Guide to the SAT II Biology—Deluxe Internet Edition
5 More Practice Tests for the SAT II Biology
SparkNotes Guide to the SAT II Chemistry—Deluxe Internet Edition
SparkNotes Guide to the SAT II U.S. History—Deluxe Internet Edition
5 More Practice Tests for the SAT II History
SparkNotes Guide to the SAT II Math Ic—Deluxe Internet Edition
5 More Practice Tests for the SAT II Math Ic
SparkNotes Guide to the SAT II Math IIc—Deluxe Internet Edition
5 More Practice Tests for the SAT II Math IIc
SparkNotes Guide to the SAT II Physics—Deluxe Internet Edition